To Martha,

Seasons of the Feminine Divine

— ❧ —

When God is shining through + glowing inside a woman, you model God as a good friend to me + many others.

Peace, Joy + Love

Carol Ann

Seasons of the Feminine Divine

Christian Feminist Prayers for the Liturgical Cycle

—— ❧ ——

MARY KATHLEEN SPEEGLE SCHMITT

CROSSROAD • NEW YORK

1993

The Crossroad Publishing Company
370 Lexington Avenue, New York, NY 10017

Printed in the United States of America

Library of Congress Cataloging-in-Publication Data

Schmitt, Mary Kathleen Speegle.
    Seasons of the feminine divine : Christian feminist prayers for
the liturgical cycle/ Mary Kathleen Speegle Schmitt.
      p. cm.
    Includes bibliographical references and index.
    ISBN 0-8245-1279-0
    1. Church year—Prayer-books and devotions—English. 2. Women—
Religious life. I. Title.
BV30.S323 1993
264'.13'092—dc20
                                          93-588
                                          CIP

TO MY MOTHER

Katherine Speegle

Contents

—— ✆ ——

Preface 13
Introduction 17
How the Prayers Were Written 29

THE PRAYERS

The Season of Advent 43
  General Prayers:
    MOTHER OF ALL CREATION   43
    WOMB OF ALL   44
    WOMANGOD WITHIN; WOMANGOD WITHOUT   45
  Advent 1: BELOVED ONE   45
  Advent 2: DIVINE BAKERWOMAN   46
  Advent 3: INHABITER OF BOTH DARK AND LIGHT   47
  Advent 4: ROCK AND GROUND   48

The Season of Christmas 50
  Christmas Eve:
    VIGILANT MOTHER   50
    ONE WHO WEEPS FOR HER LOST CHILDREN   51
  Christmas Day:
    THE FEMININE DIVINE AS HOMEMAKER   52
    DIVINE SEAMSTRESS   52
  Christmas 1: GRANDMOTHER   53
  Christmas 2: MOTHER OF THE UNIVERSE   54

The Season of Epiphany 55
    General Prayer: MOTHER EAGLE   56
    The Feast of the Epiphany: MOTHER HEN   57
    Epiphany 1 (Proper 1): MOTHER OF CREATION   58
    Epiphany 2 (Proper 2):
        ONE WHO CALLS IN THE NIGHT   58
    Epiphany 3 (Proper 3):
        WOMANGOD OUR ROCK AND SPRING   59
    Epiphany 4 (Proper 4): ROOT OF WISDOM   60
    Epiphany 5 (Proper 5): WEAVER OF THE WEB OF LIFE   61
    Epiphany 6: HEARER OF THE SLAVE GIRL   62
    Epiphany 7:
        SHEKINAH, DIVINE HEALING WOMAN,
        AND GRANDMOTHER OF THE OPPRESSED   62
    Epiphany 8:
        MOTHER OF ORPHANS   63
        ONE WHOSE LOVE IS ENOUGH   64

The Season of Lent 65
    General Prayer: PREGNANT MOTHER   66
    Ash Wednesday: DIVINE MIDWIFE   67
    Lent 1:
        WOMANGOD AS FLOOD (ONE WHO WEEPS FOR US)   68
        WOMANGOD AS RAINBOW   68
        WOMANGOD AS WILDERNESS   69
    Lent 2: MOTHER OF SARAH AND ALL HUMANITY   69
    Lent 3: MOTHER WISDOM   70
    Lent 4:
        PERSISTENT LOVER   71
        STORM-GODDESS   72
    Lent 5:
        KERNEL OF GRAIN   73
        COMPANION IN THE LONGEST NIGHT   73

Holy Week 75
   Passion Sunday: WOUNDED ONE 76
   Holy Monday: MOTHER OF ALL 77
   Holy Tuesday:
     SHADOW SISTER IN THE UNKNOWN WOMAN
     WHO ANOINTED JESUS 78
   Holy Wednesday: WOMANGOD AS STREAM 79
   Maundy Thursday:
     HOLY FOUNTAIN 80
     THE WOMEN UNNAMED AT THE LORD'S SUPPER 80
   Good Friday:
     THE GODDESS IN THE WOMEN WHO DID NOT FLEE 81
   Holy Saturday: WOMEN AT THE BURIAL OF JESUS 82

The Season of Easter 83
   General Prayer: EARTH DANCER 84
   Easter Vigil:
     SISTER WHO JOURNEYS WITH US 85
     WOMAN OF TRANSFORMING POWER 85
   Easter Day:
     MARY MAGDALENE, FIRST APOSTLE 86
     WOMEN'S EXPERIENCE OF THE EMPTY TOMB 88
   Easter 2: HEARTBEAT OF THIS EARTH 88
   Easter 3: BAKERWOMAN 89
   Easter 4: SHEPHERDESS OF THE UNIVERSE 90
   Easter 5: GODDESS OF THE LEAFY VINE 90
   Easter 6: RISEN SISTER 91
   Easter 7: DIVINE HEALING WOMAN 92
   Ascension of the Lord: BROODING SPIRIT 93

The Season of Pentecost 94
Divine Enabling One (Propers 9–13)
   General Prayer: WOMANGOD AS RIVER 96

Day of Pentecost: WOMANSPIRIT   96
Trinity Sunday:
  ONE WHO MAKES THE GROUND HOLY   97
Proper 9 (May 29–June 4): SHEKINAH   98
Proper 10 (June 5–11): AWAKENING DAWN   99
Proper 11 (June 12–18): MUSTARD SEED GODDESS   100
Proper 12 (June 19–25): WEAVER OF THE UNIVERSE   100
Proper 13 (June 26–July 2):
  GODDESS OF THE CHERUBIM   101
  DIVINE HEALING WOMAN   102

The Feminine Divine as Mature Woman
(Propers 14–20)
General Prayers:
  GODDESS OUR RIPENING   103
  VINEYARD OF OUR DELIGHT   103
Proper 14 (July 3–9):
  DEFENDER OF WOMEN AND CHILDREN   104
Proper 15 (July 10–16): INTIMATE FRIEND   105
Proper 16 (July 17–23):
  ONE WHO FEEDS THE HUNGRY   105
Proper 17 (July 24–30):
  LOVER OF OUR BODIES AND SOULS   106
Proper 18 (July 31–August 6): FRAGRANT BREAD   107
Proper 19 (August 7–13):
  YOU WHO MOVE US BEYOND BIRTH TO BIRTH   107
Proper 20 (August 14–20):
  BREAST-FEEDING MOTHER   108

Womangod as Queen of the Universe (Propers 21–27)
General Prayer: HOLY GRANDMOTHER   109
Proper 21 (August 21–27): LOVER OF CREATION   109
Proper 22 (August 28–September 3):
  GRANDMOTHER OF THE OPPRESSED   110

Proper 23 (September 4–10): HIDDEN TREASURE — 111

Proper 24 (September 11–17): POTENT WINE — 112

Proper 25 (September 18–24):
ONE WHO COMES IN LITTLE CHILDREN — 112

Proper 26 (September 25–October 1):
HEART OF COMPASSION — 113
COURAGE OF ESTHER — 113

Proper 27 (October 2–8): DIVINE WOMAN — 114

Harvest Thanksgiving: VINEYARD OF OUR DELIGHT — 115

Womangod as One Who Brings Us Home
(Propers 28–Reign of Christ)
General Prayers:
AUTUMN GODDESS — 116
WISE GRANDMOTHER — 116

Proper 28 (October 9–15): ENTICING LIFESTREAM — 117

Proper 29 (October 16–22):
ONE WHO SPEAKS TO US IN OUR BROKENNESS — 118

Proper 30 (October 23–29):
LIBERATOR OF THE DISPOSSESSED — 119

Proper 31 (October 30–November 5):
AUTHOR OF LOVE — 120

All Saints' Day: DIVINE GRANDMOTHER — 120

Proper 32 (November 6–12):
PETULANT GRANDMOTHER — 121

Proper 33 (November 13–19): ANCIENT WOMAN — 122

Proper 34 (Reign of Christ):
QUEEN OF THE UNIVERSE — 123

Bibliography — 125
Index of Biblical References — 127

Preface

___ ʖ ___

I N 1975 I EMBARKED upon a journey that eventually involved the study of feminist theology in a doctor of ministry program at St. Stephen's College, Edmonton, Canada. A friend studying at the University of California wrote to suggest that I read Mary Daly's *Beyond God the Father.* I was initially reluctant to read a book of this nature for several reasons. First, I came from a conservative pietistic church, and the ideas that Daly advanced were shocking. Second, I tended to be conservative at an emotional level, as well — reluctant to change deeply felt values. Finally, since I was living in a remote area of Canada in the nether world of mothering two toddlers, I had little energy at the time to read complex theological rhetoric.

It took at least a year before I gained the courage to go into Edmonton to order the book from New York. I joked with the clerk at the store that a book this radical might be stopped at the border. Yet the Spirit was at work in my respect for my friend and my trust in her judgment. It took almost a year for me to read the book because of the emotional upheaval Daly's thoughts evoked in me. A few years later I saw a notice of a course on "feminist theology" to be held at Iliff School of Theology in Denver. I mentioned the course to my spouse, Ed, who said we could not afford the air fare for me to attend, and, for the time, I dropped the idea. The next year I saw that the course was to be presented again and experi-

enced a deep feeling of necessity to attend. This time I wrote to
the national office of the Anglican Church of Canada inquir-
ing about scholarship funds. I was given a grant that enabled
me to attend the course taught by Carol Christ and Judith
Plaskow. For me, coming from a remote area where I had had
no one to talk to about Daly's work, plunging into a course
based on Starhawk's book *Spiral Dance* was like being thrown
into the fire. Painfully, a whole new world opened up, and my
journey was under way in earnest. About this time I moved
with my family to Edmonton, where I began to find people
with whom I could share my concerns. I became more and
more involved in study, reflection, and various group experiences with women who also sought to experience the feminine
Divine, without feeling they were transgressing the boundaries
of the Christian faith.

In the mid-1980s I undertook a dissertation project to examine how persons of Anglican, United Church of Canada,
and Roman Catholic traditions would respond to prayers
for worship that included feminine symbolism. Reports from
the Anglican tradition were mainly positive, with negative
comments from two participants. Reports from readers of
the United Church were mostly favorable. Reports from Roman Catholic theology students indicated that although they
personally saw the validity of these prayers, they doubted
such prayers would be easily accepted by the majority of
parishioners in Sunday worship. I also received many help-
ful comments on the form and phrasing of the prayers, which
have affected the ones subsequently written for this book.

I would like to thank all the people who have supported
me in the writing of this book, especially Marjorie Procter-
Smith, whose comments and wisdom have been very valuable,
and Frank Henderson, whose counsel and advice concerning
the form of the opening prayer as well as research into the

feminine divine have given essential direction to this project. I am indebted to the faculty and staff of St. Stephen's College, who created an environment that fostered the exploration of feminist theology and provided needed personal support at critical points of my journey. I also express my appreciation to the many women who have read or heard these prayers, responded with enthusiasm, and offered their insights. I am deeply grateful to my spouse, Ed, for his encouragement and support, and my children, Karl and Ursula, for their patience and love.

Introduction

—— ❧ ——

THE PURPOSE OF THIS COLLECTION OF PRAYERS is to provide an opportunity for people to engage in prayer that values women's life experience in the context of the Judeo-Christian tradition. Women's experience over the past several thousand years has been seen as that of limited and inferior beings. This perception of women's experience is particularly made clear in the Judeo-Christian tradition by the restriction of names for the Divine to masculine titles and attributes and in the exclusion of women from roles of authority in church and temple both with respect to teaching and to liturgical function. In theological reflection as well, the expression of women's experience has not been taken seriously and, more often than not, has been overlooked altogether.

The Quest for the Feminine Divine

A principal way of valuing women's experience of faith and life is through expressing names of the Divine in female images in prayer. Yet to pray to the Divine in female terms is fraught with difficulty for people of the Judeo-Christian tradition, because female deity has systematically been objectified as evil, and those persons in our history who have persisted in worshiping the Divine in female expression have been persecuted, frequently to the point of martyrdom. While no one in the Judeo-Christian tradition can reasonably challenge the biblical testimony that women are created in the image of the Divine, to take the logical step to naming the Divine with female titles and describing Her with female attributes causes considerable anxiety.

A case in point is the anxiety in Judeo-Christian circles around the use of a title like "Goddess." The very name fills many of us with dread, because we have been conditioned at a very deep level to believe the word refers to a pagan deity whose rites include abominable activities. In reality, of course, the title "Goddess" is very simply the female counterpart of the title "God." We do not tremble with fear when we hear the word "God," even though the title could easily refer to deities other than that of the Judeo-Christian tradition. In abhorring the title "Goddess" while accepting the title "God," we are falling prey to the Judeo-Christian practice of objectifying female deity as evil, with the consequent impact of devaluing female persons and roles. By avoiding the title "Goddess," we attempt to assure ourselves that we are not falling into the worship of a pagan deity. On the other hand, by using only the masculine title "God," we are unwittingly supporting the fear of the feminine Divine that has long been the source of women's oppression in both church and society.

The reality is that we cannot enter into the naming of the Divine in feminine metaphors without anxiety. Too many years of prohibitions both spoken and unspoken well up within us. Also, there are too many years of unspoken knowledge of what happened to the women and men who held out for worship of the feminine Divine in years past, and of the ridicule of persons in more recent church history who raised up in public the idea of a female aspect of the Divine. Although many feminists question the validity of the theories of Carl Jung about women, we are greatly indebted to his work in the early part of this century and to that of members of his school who, from outside of the church, began to make a case for a restoration of the feminine in religious imagery. We are also indebted to the church itself, as it has responded to the liberating Spirit of Christ in seeking to bring into reality the baptismal formula from Galatians 3:28 that promises that in Christ there is "no longer Jew or Greek, there is no longer slave or free, there is no longer male and female; for all of you are one in Christ Jesus."

The Feminine Divine in the Judeo-Christian Tradition

To some it may come as a surprise, that, despite the Judeo-Christian tradition's negative and even punitive attitude toward the worship of the feminine Divine, female names and attributes have persisted in this tradition from biblical times to the recent past. Rafael Patai identifies manifestations of the Divine perceived in Hebrew Scripture and tradition as feminine, such as the Shekinah (numinous Presence or Glory), Hokmah (Wisdom), and the Cherubim (ecstatic Love).[1]

Virginia Ramey Mollenkott shows that there are many female expressions of the Divine in the Bible that have been either overlooked or glossed over by previous generations of interpreters.[2] Images described by Mollenkott include Birth-giving Woman, Nursing Mother, Mother, Mother Bear, Mother Eagle, Mother Hen, Midwife, Homemaker, Baker-woman, Female Companion, and Female Beloved.

Elaine Pagels in *The Gnostic Gospels* outlines evidence that in the early church some communities experienced and addressed the Divine as female.[3] Elisabeth Schüssler Fiorenza in *In Memory of Her: A Feminist Theological Reconstruc-*

---

1. Rafael Patai, *The Hebrew Goddess* (New York: KTAV, 1967): Shekinah and Hokmah, 137–56; Cherubim, 121–36.

2. Virginia Ramey Mollenkott, *The Divine Feminine: the Biblical Imagery of God as Female* (New York: Crossroad, 1984).

3. Elaine Pagels, *The Gnostic Gospels* (New York: Random House, 1979).

tion of Christian Origins joins Pagels in pointing out that in
these communities strong women similar to Mary Magdalene,
Priscilla, and Lydia carried important leadership roles, both
liturgical and administrative.[4] Pagels and Schüssler Fiorenza
describe the gradual elimination of both female leadership and
the expression of the Divine in female images in the first several centuries of church history, although very limited use of
female images continued. In the patristic period, for example,
there were still references to Jesus as Breast-feeding Mother,
which continued into the Middle Ages.[5]

   It is not surprising that after the suppressing of the feminine Divine in the early church veneration of the mother of
Jesus began to develop. In the emergence of doctrines such
as the immaculate conception, perpetual virginity, and bodily
assumption Mary was given Goddess qualities. Titles such as
"Queen of Heaven and Earth" were derived from titles for the
Hebrew Goddess and echo the traits of deities from Hellenistic cultures. For instance, Hellenistic goddesses were called
"Virgin" (meaning self-contained rather than sexually unini-
tiated); the sorrows of Mary recall those of Demeter mourning
the loss of her daughter Persephone; and qualities assigned to
Mary like skill at weaving and her connection with the dove
and the moon connect her with Athena and other Goddess
images.[6] In the Middle Ages mystical writers such as Hildegard of Bingen and Julian of Norwich named the Divine in the
feminine. Some of these names are explicit, such as "Mother
Jesus,"[7] while others are implicit, expressing divine incarna-

---

   4. Elisabeth Schüssler Fiorenza, *In Memory of Her: A Feminist Theological
Reconstruction of Christian Origins* (New York: Crossroad, 1984).
   5. Mollenkott, *The Divine Feminine*, 20–25.
   6. Joan C. Engelsman, *The Feminine Dimension of the Divine* (Philadelphia:
Westminster Press, 1979), 122–33.
   7. Brendan Doyle, ed., *Meditations with Julian of Norwich* (Santa Fe: Bear &
Company, 1983), 101; see also 85, 90, 106, and 132 for other references to the Divine
as Mother.

tion in images drawn from nature; for instance, the divine Presence is perceived in the "greening" of the earth, and nature in the symbolic system is often equated with the feminine.[8]

Thus, in the Judeo-Christian tradition there has been a continuous presence of the feminine Divine until relatively recently. To think of the Divine in feminine terms is not new, and to seek new names to express our experience of the Divine is a valid part of the human-divine dialogue that is central to worship. An important part of finding new names for the Divine is to clarify to ourselves that there is no single name for the Divine — indeed, that a title such as "Father" is but one metaphor for the Divine, albeit one much used in recent years. Sallie McFague has pointed out the danger of literalizing our concept of the Divine. By emphasizing one or two names or using a few names almost exclusively, we restrict our perception of the Divine and essentially block the growth that is basic to the human-divine encounter.[9]

The Relation of the Judeo-Christian and Ancient Goddess Traditions

It is important to examine the original antagonism between Judaism and female deity. Studies in the last century suggest that life in matriarchal societies that centered around Goddess worship was positive and benevolent in many respects. Great civilizations grew up under its tutelage. Many achievements since attributed to men, such as the development of written

---

8. This image is drawn from Hildegard of Bingen, who sees God present in the intensity of creation: "Glance at the sun. See the moon and the stars. Gaze at the beauty of earth's greenings. Now, think. What delight God gives to humankind with all these things. Who gives all these shining, wonderful gifts, if not God?" (Gabriele Uhlein, ed., *Meditations with Hildegard of Bingen* [Santa Fe: Bear & Company, 1983], 45).

9. Sallie McFague, *Metaphorical Theology: Models of God in Religious Language* (Philadelphia: Fortress Press, 1982).

language and systematic law, occurred in societies that worshiped the Goddess. Women were often educated and gifted leaders and thinkers. Sir Arthur Evans, in excavating the site at Knossos (Crete), suggested that these matriarchal communities were peaceful rather than warlike (their cities had no walls),[10] although Merlin Stone in *When God Was a Woman*, reports evidence of female warriors.[11] Certainly, Goddess religion, which was based on women's biological cycles and connection to nature, offers us a picture of the Divine that is missing today.

Both Judaism and Christianity, however, defined themselves over and against Goddess worship in the Middle East, in Europe, and eventually in the Americas and other parts of the world. That is, in order to gain authority over the people, leaders in these religious (and political) groups felt compelled to objectify Goddess worship as evil and identified it with Satan and witchcraft. By objectifying the Goddess as evil, women, too, because of their connection to the Goddess by physical resemblance, became suspect as ones who sabotaged the new religions — and rightly so, because women did not easily give up the deep meaning and connection with the Divine that Goddess worship had afforded them. (We remember, for instance, how the biblical Rachel carried the family idols with her when she accompanied Jacob to their new home.) It took centuries and many martyrs of the Goddess religion to achieve the supremacy of a male God and to destroy the heritage of a once noble religion and civilization that was in many respects little worse and in some ways better than those that replaced it.

It is tempting, therefore, for women alienated in the Judeo-

---

10. A basis for the assertion that the cities had no walls relates to the excavation of the ruins of the palace at Knossos; however, other archaeologists dispute Evans's theory.

11. Merlin Stone, *When God Was a Woman* (New York: Harcourt Brace Jovanovich, 1976), 3–4, 34–35, 45–47.

Christian tradition to idealize ancient Goddess religion and
to objectify patriarchy and all men as the source of evil.
The evil that women have experienced has been intense. It
is important to reflect, however, on what male experience
in matriarchal society might have been like. No matter how
benevolent and nonviolent the leaders of those societies were,
it is questionable how much insight they had into the male
role and experience in that society. It is not impossible that
the movement to male dominance arose out of a quest to
emancipate subordinate males in a female system. While not
justifying the incredible violence of the movement, the extent
of that violence may be testimony to the intensity of the male
experience of exclusion, and the inclusion of compassion as
a central theme in an otherwise imperialistic male movement
may stem from men's memory of their own oppression.

It is not the purpose of this book, therefore, to eliminate
male imagery and experience from the prayer of the church.
Whether the Divine is seen as exclusively male or as exclusively female, the image is incomplete. For this reason I am
attracted to Patai's suggestion that the Cherubim in the Holy
of Holies in the Jewish Temple were composed of the image
of a male and a female figure in ecstatic embrace — an image
of wholeness.[12] Anything less than this wholeness blocks our
relationship with the Divine. God is male and female, and at
the same time neither male nor female. Yet until we use female images, women and men are deprived of a connection
with the feminine aspect of the Divine and a vision of divine
wholeness. Until we balance the one-sided symbolic system
of the Judeo-Christian tradition, we cannot begin to understand what full humanity is, and our vision of the meaning of
Christian community remains partial and defective.

---

12. Patai, *The Hebrew Goddess*, 59–98.

The "Maleness" of Jesus Christ

A major obstacle for many women who are becoming sensitive to the feminine Divine is the maleness of the second person of the Trinity. Jesus as a historical person was known as male, and in that part of the Christian tradition in which Jesus has been understood as a heroic figure, he has been experienced as male. When Jesus is given the name of the first person of the Trinity, "Lord," we may experience him as a male potentate who supports and validates male authority and the male power structure, and in certain periods of history he was definitely interpreted in this way. Christ as Servant-King suggests a different order from that of the dominant male-oriented structure, but in practice the latter continues to prevail.

Feminist theologians who have remained within the tradition, however, see Jesus as Liberator rather than Lord. Although it was unthinkable in Jesus' society, they point out, for a man to speak to a woman in public, Jesus did so many times. He not only spoke to women; he entered into dialogue with women and learned from them, for example, in his interaction with the Syro-Phoenician woman (Mark 7:24–30). Women, not only poor women but women of high position in the society of that time, were among his faithful followers. It was to a woman that Jesus first appeared and to women that the resurrection was first announced. Jesus clearly had an understanding and compassion for women that was remarkable for a man of his time.

Stephen Mitchell points out that, whatever one believes about the virgin birth of Jesus, in the eyes of the public Jesus appeared to be illegitimate. In Mark 6:1–6 Jesus was not called the son of his father, as would normally have been the case, but rather the "son of Mary," indicating public belief that he was not Joseph's son.[13] This perception meant that both Jesus and his mother would have been ostracized in his home community of Nazareth. If this is an accurate picture of what happened, such suffering would have opened him to compassion for other oppressed and victimized people, and the suffering of his mother would have opened his eyes and heart to much that women suffer.

A case might be made that it was good that Jesus was male. As a male his willingness to give up his place of dominance, aligning himself with the poor, the oppressed, the widows and orphans, provides a model to men and to women who benefit by connection with men of power. Through the example of Jesus we are called to relinquish our share of power over others and become part of the work of the church in empowering the dispossessed.

In the larger picture of things it does not matter now whether the historical Jesus was male. It does matter that Jesus' maleness has been used for centuries to oppress women and continues to be used in this way today. At the same time, the One we call the Christ is more than the historical Jesus. The One we call the Christ, the One who was before all time and who will be forever, is Logos, a masculine concept drawn from the Wisdom tradition of Judaism. Because Logos was understood as the feminine Hokmah, it is valid to see Christ as a manifestation of Wisdom, or Sophia.

Elisabeth Schüssler Fiorenza supports the connection between Jesus and Divine Wisdom. She suggests that the Divine depicted by Jesus through parable and deed, the "God of graciousness and goodness who accepts everyone and brings about justice and well-being for everyone without exception"

---

13. Stephen Mitchell, *The Gospel according to Jesus: A New Translation and Guide to His Essential Teachings for Believers and Unbelievers* (New York: Harper-Collins, 1991), 19–28.

is the divine Sophia, the One who wills the wholeness and humanity of everyone and therefore enabled the Jesus movement to become a "discipleship of equals."[14]

Wisdom and incarnation are closely linked. Christ lives not only in that other world we call heaven, but within the human race. We find Christ wherever we find any human being suffering. We touch the wounds of Christ whenever we receive the suffering ones and minister in Christ's name. We find Christ in the church, in love and forgiveness and honesty and openness. We experience the caring and strengthening of Christ in friendships that are based on generosity and sharing. We touch the body of Christ in the physical contact we share in the Peace in the Sunday liturgy. Eating Christ's body in the bread of the Eucharist, we become the actual Body of Christ. Clearly in all of these instances Christ is neither male nor female and yet both. Whatever gender Christ experienced in the flesh has been transcended and Christ now is available to all in whatever form is needed.

For women who have suffered oppression, an important source of grace is reconnecting to other women, becoming part of what feminists call "the sisterhood." This touching and connecting and sharing of experiences restores women's belief in their own experience of reality, their own potential as human beings, and the dignity and beauty of their physical bodies. This connecting with other women is a Christ-experience. Women experience Christ in the love and acceptance and validation they receive from other women who have suffered as they have suffered. This is not to say that women cannot experience Christ in relationship with men; they can and do. For many women who have been deeply wounded in their relationships with men, however, the grace

---

14. Schüssler Fiorenza, *In Memory of Her,* 130, 135.

is more likely to be received, at least initially, through other women.

Toward a Vision of Wholeness: Shalom

What we are talking about in this collection of prayers has to do with a vision of Shalom, that eternal community in which the baptismal formula from Galatians 3:28 mentioned above is a reality — what Elisabeth Schüssler Fiorenza calls "a discipleship of equals." For Shalom to happen in our lives, it is essential to meet the divine Goddess who is one and the same as the God we have known and yet who has been and continues to be hidden from us. Opening to the feminine Divine enables vast new possibilities for peace and justice in this frail world and among the vulnerable peoples who inhabit it.

It is time to bring the female way of being out of the shadow. All the while the male way of being has reigned supreme there has been a female presence, but that presence is a shadow presence — felt but not known fully. As long as the feminine is experienced as shadow, terrible oppression of women — as in the execution of "witches" in the Reformation and later — will continue to occur. Ironically, anti-"pagans" often justify repudiation of the ancient Goddess religion by condemning the practice of human sacrifice in matriarchal societies. As we look at the modern male-oriented faiths today, with wars and racism and the oppression of women, how many millions of human sacrifices do we see? How many more do we need to demonstrate that something deep is missing?

How the Prayers Were Written

———— ❧ ————

ACCORDING TO MARJORIE PROCTER-SMITH there are three ways to include women in the male-oriented language of the Judeo-Christian liturgical tradition: nonsexist, inclusive, and emancipatory.[1] The nonsexist approach avoids mention of gender — "humanity" instead of "mankind." The inclusive approach balances male and female images. The emancipatory approach challenges stereotypical use of male and female references and attempts to transform liturgical language.

While each approach makes a positive contribution to the reformation of religious language, each also has its negative aspects. While the nonsexist approach is the least disruptive, often the neutral words used are still heard as "male" because of the mentality of the worshipers. The inclusive approach addresses this lack by the inclusion of female gender references: "sisters and brothers" instead of "humankind," names of women in the tradition alongside those of men, and feminine titles and pronouns for the Divine. The negative aspect of the inclusive approach arises from the common perception that anything female is inferior to that which is male, and there are negative connotations for almost any female title or attribute that can be used to balance the male images: "Lady," "Queen," "Mistress," etc. There are definite prejudices against the whole concept of "Mother"

---

1. Marjorie Procter-Smith, *In Her Own Rite: Constructing Feminist Liturgical Tradition* (Nashville: Abingdon Press, 1990), 59–84.

because of social attitudes about motherhood. Emancipatory language attempts to claim the terms that have been derogatory and to value what has been devalued in our language. A theological basis for this approach to language is the belief that the Divine is embodied in the struggle of women against oppression. The goal of emancipatory language, Procter-Smith goes on to say, is to make women, who have been invisible in the Judeo-Christian tradition, visible and valued members of the religious communities of which they are a part.

This collection of prayers attempts to be emancipatory in approach. I do not claim to have achieved this goal perfectly, as we all have our blind spots, and I am far from being exempt from such blindness. These prayers, rather, represent a reaching out to the feminine Divine. My concern is not to be politically correct but to establish a dialogue with the Divine that comes from a place of integrity within my own experience. As women's experiences vary, it is quite possible that not all the prayers will speak to all women.

Narrative and Poetic Form

These prayers are designed so that they may be used as opening prayers of the liturgy. Opening prayers, or "collects," set the theme related to the Scripture readings for a particular day. These prayers have traditionally addressed the Divine in abstract statements of praise and petition that are philosophical or doctrinal in nature. While there are strengths in this approach, the weakness is that the prayer images may remain at an intellectual level rather than acting as agents to draw worshipers into the concrete ongoing story of the divine-human encounter.

Helen Kathleen Hughes explores an alternative view of the

opening prayer by suggesting a narrative form.[2] When the prayer is narrative, the Divine is described in concrete rather than abstract actions. The prayer opens with a narrative basis on which a petition may be made. The narrative moves from status quo, to crisis, to resolution, so that each prayer is a complete story that connects with the larger story of the faith. Hughes points out that it is less the words and concepts that connect the worshiping community with the "deep meaning" of the prayer than the movement of the narrative elements that draw the hearers into the continuing story.[3] Because this story is ongoing, the prayers are open-ended, the resolution being bound up in the future reign of the Divine. In this way the prayer narrative "invites transformation" because the people praying participate in the prayer action rather than simply hearing and reflecting on ideas in a detached way.[4]

The prayers in this book attempt to follow a narrative style to enable those praying to move more deeply into the drama of the story of the faith. Some of the story action is drawn from biblical stories and some is imaginative, drawn intuitively from the images in Scripture.

The Images

Many of the names used for the Divine in both the addresses of these prayers and in the ascriptions at the ends of the prayers are metaphorical images drawn from female experience, from the female body cycle, and from nature, with which woman's body has a deep cyclical connection. For some, these nature images and images drawn from the female cycle suggest "pa-

2. Helen Kathleen Hughes, "The Opening Prayer of the Sacramentary: A Structural Study of the Easter Cycle," dissertation, University of Notre Dame (Ann Arbor, Mich.: University Microfilms International, 1981), 310, 324, 329, 343.

3. Hughes, "The Opening Prayer of the Sacramentary," 129–45.

4. Hughes, "The Opening Prayer of the Sacramentary," 287–300.

ganism" and "fertility" religion against which Judaism and Christianity have defined themselves. Yet it is precisely in defining ourselves over and against what is female and the feminine Divine that we have created within ourselves the dualistic split that prevents us today from finding wholeness in relationship with the Divine.

The Divine did not magically emerge with the appearance of Abraham or Moses; She was already present and active in the world. What developed from the Divine as encountered by Abraham and Moses was the move to understanding the Divine as One Being and the innovative giving of masculine titles and attributes to the Divine: that is, recognizing that men, too, are in the image of God. Reclaiming Goddess imagery and titles, therefore, is not anti-God. Such reclamation is simply reminding ourselves that the One whom we call God was known in earlier times as Goddess and understood with female traits. Such names, therefore, while seeming alien because of the deep entrenchment over the past several thousand years of the notion of female as evil, are not names of another God. There is One God(dess) and One alone, although in many manifestations.

While some of the names used in the prayers in this book are female images of the Divine drawn directly from the Bible, others are not biblical in the sense that they are found verbatim in the Bible. Many of the images are suggested by metaphors in Scripture that have connection with traditionally perceived categories of femaleness such as nature and represent the extraction of the hidden feminine dimension of the Divine. Some images are drawn from the works of Christian spirituality in postbiblical times that relate to the readings of the day. All of them reflect woman's creation in the image of the Divine and the theology of the Incarnation. In this sense, all of the images are biblical.

Some of the prayers refer to roles symbolically female, although the references could be male as well. "Weaver," for instance, refers to women's view of the interconnectedness of the universe as compared to the dominant society's emphasis on individual achievement and competition; yet there have been and are male weavers.

The ascriptions at the conclusion of the prayers, normally references to the Trinity as mediated through Christ, are again evocative rather than doctrinal statements. Often three persons or images are mentioned, but sometimes two or four, indicating that there are many names for the Divine and that by naming more than one name, we are expressing the unity of the Divine rather than a mathematical dissection of divine nature.

Sometimes the second person of the Trinity, Jesus Christ, is named in the feminine to express the androgynous character of Christ's work as Liberator of the oppressed and to name the connection between Christ and the feminine Wisdom of Hebrew tradition. It is important to understand that in using a female symbol I am not making a statement about the historicity of Jesus, however intriguing a possibility that might be. I am talking about the contemporaneous and eternal Christ who, by the power of the resurrection, transcends gender. This Christ, who is one and the same with the historical Jesus and yet far more vast in our experience, meets and transforms us in myriad ways and, I suspect, far more than we recognize.[5]

Many of the images, rather than referring to female anatomy or roles understood as female, reflect the "feminine" as understood in Jungian psychology. However, no presumption is made here that psychological difference between male

---

5. See Christin Lore Weber, *WomanChrist: A New Vision of Feminist Spirituality* (San Francisco: Harper & Row, 1985).

and female is scientifically true. Differences observed by Jung and those of his school may well not have been the result of any "natural" differences but due to the oppression of women and the resultant culture of subordination as described by Jean Baker Miller.[6] These prayers attempt to revalue what has been devalued because of association with femaleness and ancient female-oriented religion. Earth and nature are revalued as the Body of the Divine. Body and self are revalued in contrast with the dominant values of spirit and the giving up of self. Self-giving as a virtue is reserved by and large for the part of the cycle in which persons have approached a stage of maturity and are able to give without endangering their centeredness in Christ.[7] The positive elements of darkness are revalued. It is important to remember that in the desert climate of the Bible, shadow and darkness could be saving forces in the cause of human survival and the force of the sun could be deadly. Human emotion is revalued where reason and the exertion of will over emotion have been given dominance in Christian theology. The purpose of revaluing the shadow side of our religious imagery is not to superimpose female values over male, but to move to integration and wholeness.

Some of the prayers depict the experience of women (for instance, barrenness), and some particular experiences of women in the Bible or church tradition (for example, women at the foot of the cross).

In a number of prayers I have used the title "Woman" as a name of the Divine. This title has been drawn from the

---

6. Jean Baker Miller, *Toward a New Psychology of Women* (Boston: Beacon Press, 1976), 3–26.

7. See Valerie Saiving, "The Human Situation: A Feminine View," in *Womanspirit Rising: A Feminist Reader,* Carol Christ and Judith Plaskow, eds. (San Francisco: Harper & Row, 1979), 25–42, for insight into how male-oriented Christian principles such as self-sacrifice may be harmful to subordinate groups such as women.

mythology of North American aboriginal peoples who speak of Her as "Old Woman." It is important to realize that this expression was metaphorical and not intended to suggest that the divine was a literal old woman. Although my understanding of aboriginal mythology and religion is limited, I suspect that the "Old Woman," although separate from the Manitou, was also experienced as a manifestation of the Great Spirit. Such separation is not necessarily unlike the Christian belief that the human Jesus is an expression of the One Divinity. By calling the Divine "Old Woman," two objectives are achieved. The first is the recognition that the feminine Divine is incarnate in women; to speak of Divinity's womanhood is not unlike speaking of Christ's manhood or of "Christ in us." The second objective is the revaluing of older women, who in our society are often excluded or devalued because of the emphasis upon youthfulness. Yet anyone who relates very much to older women finds frequently a delightful sagacity and a generosity that give deeper meaning to our understanding of what it is to be human. One of my formative experiences of the presence of the Divine came through my great-aunt Nona, whose deep acceptance of me enabled a comprehension of divine Love that otherwise I might not have had for years. She was one of the few people who knew and blessed that inner core of myself — a blessing that enabled growth and transformation as time went on. When I have used the title "Woman," the whole range of my great-aunts and many other women has been in my mind's eye as beloved persons through whom the Divine Spirit became incarnate for me.

While I use a variety of names for the feminine Divine, I have not shied away from speaking, on occasion, of the One we have known by the name of "God" as "Goddess." When using this title, I refer to the Hebrew Goddess, of whom few of us have heard until very recently, but who has always been present in various manifestations in the Judeo-Christian tradition.

Rafael Patai suggests that the real history of the people of Israel was one of clinging actively to the worship of Asherah and other manifestations of the Goddess.[8] Using a tool of study similar to Schüssler Fiorenza's "hermeneutic of suspicion," Patai points out that if the persistent worship of Canaanite and other goddesses were not a reality, it would not have been necessary for prophets to bewail idolatry or for rulers to carry out bloody reforms against idolatrous activities. This reality was obscured by an interpretive overlay of the history of Israel by redactors in postexilic times. Thus, while the biblical story testifies to a small and emerging new perception of the Divine, it also obscures the presence in Judaism of concurrent worship of the Goddess, quite possibly understood as Yahweh's wife, which with the move to monotheism was gradually released for a higher vision of the Divine as One. Yet this One was depicted in the Holy of Holies in this later period of development as both male and female in the quasi-human forms of the Cherubim in embrace. That is to say, the perception of the Divine as Goddess was not left behind, but rather incorporated into the new understanding of Divine Being.

It is important to observe that Goddess religion was not anti-God but a reaching out for the Divine that evolved from female perceptions in ancient matriarchal societies. Although limited in historical perspective, these had validity in their own time as divine-human encounter. To speak of the Divine as "Goddess" is not to return to an earlier stage of religious development or to idolatry, but to recognize and name the deep influence those early perceptions of the Divine as female have had and continue to have on the Judeo-Christian under-

---

8. Rafael Patai, *The Hebrew Goddess* (New York: KTAV, 1967), 34–35, 101–36.

standing of the Divine — and to reclaim the positive aspects of those perceptions. Just as we would not wish to return to worship the Divine through the ancient Israelite understanding of a God of jealous wrath who ordered the massacre of countless peoples or through the God of an empire of Christendom that ordered the massacre of countless more, we would also find it inappropriate to return to Goddess worship of a much earlier stage of human development. At the same time, there are values from the religion of that period that are valid and needful as our own understanding of justice and the will of the Divine evolves and leads us past the blindness of our own time to a deeper and fuller perception of Who the Holy One is and of who we are called to be as the church today.

Recognizing that speaking the word "Goddess" can create anxiety because of its unfamiliarity to us and the connotations that the name evokes, I suggest that if persons and groups using this book find that the title creates too much anxiety, they use another name for the Divine. On the other hand, for many persons the use of the title "Goddess" will become freeing. For some, it will be useful to use the title even if they feel uncomfortable, as a way of challenging the misogynism and self-hatred we still carry deep inside us.

A Developmental Cycle of Prayer

The prayers in this book are organized according to a developmental pattern something in the vein of Penelope Washbourn's cycle of female experience.[9] The assumption is that the Goddess is experienced mainly as Mother in Advent, Christmas, and Epiphany; as Mother Who Lets Us Go and Shadow Sister in Lent; as Wounded Sister and Sorrowful Mother in Holy

---

9. Penelope Washbourn, *Becoming Woman: The Quest for Wholeness in Female Experience* (New York: Harper & Row, 1977).

Week; as Soul Sister and Alluring Wisdom in Easter; and as embodied in mature woman in Pentecost (Enabler, Ripening One, Queen of the Universe, and One Who Brings Us Home). In this context, a number of the prayers reflect process rather than fall-redemption theology.

How These Prayers May Be Used

The prayers in this collection are intended for a variety of uses. Groups wishing to worship the Divine using prayers with explicit female or feminine imagery might find some of these prayers appropriate for their purpose. The prayers are appropriate for retreat weekends in which the feminine Divine is being explored by women only or by women and men. The prayers can also be used for personal devotions or meditation. There might be congregations interested in exploring the feminine Divine by using some of these prayers from time to time as opening prayers or collects in the Sunday worship. While some of the prayers refer generally to a liturgical season, most of them are derived from some aspect of the lectionary texts for particular Sundays throughout the church year based on the Common Lectionary — with some adaptations to the Episcopal (U.S.), Lutheran, and Roman Catholic variations of this lectionary and to the Revised Common Lectionary. Where there is not agreement among the various lections for a given day, alternative prayers relating to themes of the differing lections are suggested. For example, on Christmas 1 the Common, Revised Common, Lutheran, and Roman Catholic lectionaries cite Luke 1:22–40 as the Gospel reading, whereas the Gospel cited in the Episcopal lectionary is John 1:1–18. In this instance, reference to an alternative prayer based on John 1:1–18 is given.

For congregations interested in using the prayers in Sunday

worship, preparation is vital unless the people are already aware of issues of female language for the Divine. To use the prayers without such preparation would be detrimental to their purpose of enabling people of the faith to open to this dimension of the Divine.

For those who already worship the Divine through feminine expression, I hope that these prayers will be a small offering of additional insights. For persons or groups new to relating to the Divine through feminine expression, welcome to the journey. This journey is not easy. Our indoctrination against the very concept of the Divine as female has reached us at very deep levels. At the same time, the rewards of this pilgrimage can be profound and opening. May She bless you in this journey.

The Prayers

The Season of Advent

—— ✌ ——

I N ADVENT we experience the feminine Divine as PREGNANT MOTHER, discovering the divine earthiness within us and all humanity.

She is Creatress manifest as EARLY WINTER, emerging in the flurries of the first snow. We experience Her in moonlight shining whitely through frosty mists and in ice-laden clouds that hide the stars and moon from sight. We discern Her as darkness, but a pregnant darkness.... In Advent we are as fetal children in the Womb of the Mother. Our Mother is remote yet known, untried yet trusted, immanent, nurturing, containing, sustaining, encompassing, incubating, warm(ing). She is All-in-all from whom we cannot distinguish ourselves although we long to see her face.

General Prayers

MOTHER OF ALL CREATION

- "...a Christian's will must enter completely into its mother."

- "This Word is our eternal mother in whose body we are begotten and nourished."[1]

❧   Mother of All Creation,
     in the universe, your Womb,
     we are sustained as of one body with You.
     Protect us by your fierce love,
     and assure us that we are safe with You:
     that we radiate the strength and warmth
         of your nearness to all the world;
     One of Beauty,
     Love-Child,
     Spirit of Hope and Joy. Amen.

WOMB OF ALL

❧   Womb of All,[2]
     in the midst of a failing world
     You draw us into community with You
         and one another.
     Contain us with the faithfulness
         of your motherly-compassion:[3]
     that, nurtured by your care,
         we mother all who are in need
         of groundedness in You.

---

1. Jacob Boehme, *The Way to Christ,* trans. Peter C. Erb (New York: Paulist Press 1978), 140, 112, as quoted in Virginia Ramey Mollenkott, *The Divine Feminine: The Biblical Imagery of God as Female* (New York: Crossroad, 1984), 18–19.

2. The title "Womb of All" was drawn from Linda Clark, Marian Ronan, and Eleanor Walker, *Image-Breaking Image-Building: A Handbook for Creative Worship with Women of Christian Tradition* (New York: Pilgrim Press, 1981), 69.

3. For insight into how the Hebrew word for "mercy" or "compassion" comes from the root word for "womb," and is translated "motherly-compassion" by Phyllis Trible, see her book *God and the Rhetoric of Sexuality* (Philadelphia: Fortress Press, 1978), 31–59.

Birth-giver of the earth and skies
    and all that is,
You are one Divinity, now and forever.
Amen.

WOMANGOD WITHIN; WOMANGOD WITHOUT

Womangod within,
Womangod without,
You stir your womb to life
and are the fire within the womb.
Conceive in us the knowledge
    of our unity with You:
that, encompassed by your love,
we enter into life with warmth and joy.
Mother and Child,
You are One Divinity now and forever.
Amen.

Advent 1

BELOVED ONE

- "Where are your zeal and your might? The yearning of your heart and your compassion...are withheld from me." (Isaiah 63:15, NRSV)

- "I sought him whom my soul loves...but found him not." (Song of Solomon 3:1, NRSV)

- "All desire leads to God." (Bernard of Clairvaux)[4]

---

4. Bernard of Clairvaux, *On the Love of God* (London: A. R. Mowbray & Co. Limited, 1961), 13.

❧   Beloved One,
      our need is your gift of grace to us;
      for, knowing that all desire leads to You,
            we long for our truest Lover.
      Inspire us with your goodness and beauty:
      that, in partnership with You,
      we share in bringing into being
      the Divine Soul of the universe;
      Heart's Desire,
      Passionate One,
      Bringer of Joy. Amen.

Alternative Prayer for Advent 1 related to Isaiah 64:1–9:
"Hidden Treasure" (p. 111).

Advent 2

DIVINE BAKERWOMAN

- Levelling as justice: "Every valley shall be lifted up, and every
  mountain and hill be made low.... Then the glory of the Lord
  shall be revealed." (Isaiah 40:4–5, NRSV)
- "The kingdom of heaven is like yeast that a woman took
  and mixed in with three measures of flour until all of it was
  leavened." (Matthew 13:33; Luke 13:20–21, NRSV)

❧   Divine Bakerwoman,[5]
      your leaven in the disparities of this world
      is justice for all creation.

---

5. The image of "Bakerwoman" was, to my knowledge, introduced by Alla
Bozarth-Campbell in her prayer by the same title in *In God's Image: Toward Wholeness for Women and Men*, ed. LaVonne Althouse and Lois K. Snook (Division for
Mission in North America, Lutheran Church in America, 1976), 13, and in Clark et
al., *Image-Breaking Image-Building*, 70–71. The image is further discussed by Virginia Ramey Mollenkott in *The Divine Feminine: The Biblical Imagery of God as
Female* (New York: Crossroad, 1984), 79–82.

Make us the yeast in the rising dough
   of your universe:
that earth and heaven become one in You,
and all humanity celebrate with joy
the perpetual feast of your Peace;
Shaper of the World,
Earth Hands,[6]
Life-giving Fragrance. Amen.

Advent 3

INHABITER OF BOTH DARK AND LIGHT

- "In the beginning God created heaven and earth. Now the earth was a formless void, there was darkness over the deep, with a divine wind sweeping over the waters. God said, 'Let there be light,' and there was light.... God called light 'day,' and darkness he called 'night.'" (Genesis 1:1–5, NJB)

- John the Baptist "was not the light, but he came to testify to the light. The true light, which enlightens everyone, was coming into the world." (John 1:8–9, NRSV)

   Inhabiter of both Dark and Light,
   You take us once more into yourself,
   the Womb of all creation,
   where nothing is understood,
   but all is known.
   Reveal to us the wholeness
   promised in Christ before all time:
   that, rooted in the soil
      of your unconditional love,

---

6. "I am your rising bread, well-kneaded by some divine and knotty pair of knuckles, by your warm earth-hands..." (Alla Bozarth-Campbell, *In God's Image*, 13).

we go forth to proclaim with joy
the gospel of his coming;
Evening Star,
Rising Sun,
Energy that Shimmers throughout Time.
Amen.

Advent 4

ROCK AND GROUND

- "You were unmindful of the Rock that bore you; you forgot the God who gave you birth." (Deuteronomy 32:18, NRSV)
- "The angel said to her, 'The Holy Spirit will come upon you, and the power of the Most High will overshadow you; therefore the child to be born will be holy.' " (Luke 1:35, NRSV)
- "And I will appoint a place for my people Israel and will plant them, so that they may live in their own place, and be disturbed no more." (2 Samuel 7:10, NRSV)

    You Who Are Rock and Ground,[7]
the very soil shimmers
with the inner brilliance of your love,
and leafless trees, bared in wintry death,
shine red with the knowledge of your coming.[8]
You move within vast mountains to alter
   their shapes,
and surge in spring torrents to bring water
  to the land.
As we rest dormant in the mystery of your love,

---

7. See Paul Tillich, *Systematic Theology*, vol. 1 (Chicago: University of Chicago Press, 1951), for the concept of the Divine as the "Ground of Being."

8. See Gabriele Uhlein, ed., *Meditations with Hildegard of Bingen* (Santa Fe: Bear & Company, 1983), for Hildegard of Bingen's incarnational sense of the Divine.

direct us with your fertile power
    toward new birth:
that all heaven and earth emerge
into the full radiance of your grace;
Thou, Brooding Spirit,
New-born Child,
One Who Gives Birth to Thoughts Conceived.
Amen.

The Season of Christmas

———— ❧ ————

I N CHRISTMAS we know the feminine Divine as BIRTH-GIVING MOTHER. She is embodied in Mary the Mother of Jesus, the Christ-bearer, who gives birth to the Hope of the World.

She is the Creatress, who brings the universe to life.

She is the Source of All, the One who has conceived each and all of us before the foundation of time, and who has, through our biological mothers, brought us into this world.

She is the One who is present with us in each passage of life, each new birth, guiding and strengthening us and bringing us ever nearer to the Radiance of her face.

Christmas Eve

VIGILANT MOTHER

- The description of the watchmen on the walls of Jerusalem evokes the image of Lady Wisdom in Proverbs 31, the vigilant Mother who never sleeps. (Isaiah 62:6–7, 10–12)

❧   Vigilant Mother,
You who never sleep

but cradle your drowsing Child
in the protective curve of your arm,
give us the strength
to pray unceasingly for peace,
and to live out our prayers
by seeking to bring justice
to those who suffer and are oppressed:
that every obstacle to Shalom be removed,
and all humanity pass through your gates
   into Glory.
Spirit of Love and Truth,
You are One Divinity for all times.
Amen.

ONE WHO WEEPS FOR HER LOST CHILDREN

- "Let the earth rejoice! ... the daughters of Judah exult, because of your judgments, Yahweh. ... Light dawns for the upright, and joy for honest hearts." (Psalm 97:1, 8, 11, NJB)
- "For the yoke of their burden, and ... the rod of their oppressor, you have broken. ... For a child has been born for us, ... and he is named ... Prince of Peace." (Isaiah 9:4–6, NRSV)

   One Who Weeps for her lost children,
at your promise of justice
in a world full of oppression and sorrow,
the daughters of Judah danced and sang.
Soften our hearts with the tears
   of your compassion:
that hope, born anew within us,
issue in acts of justice and mercy.
Sorrowful Mother,
Child of Promise,
and Spirit of Peace,

You are the Divine One-in-Three forever.
Amen.

Christmas Day

THE FEMININE DIVINE AS HOMEMAKER

- "In the beginning was the Word, and the Word was with God, and the Word was God." (John 1:1, NRSV)
- Following the theme of Word or Wisdom: "The truly capable woman — who can find her? She is far beyond the price of pearls.... She gets up while it is still dark giving her household their food, giving orders to her serving girls.... She holds out her hands to the poor, she opens her arms to the needy." (Proverbs 31:10–31, NJB)

💕   Maker of this earth our home,
You sweep the heavens
with your starry skirt of night
and polish the eastern sky
to bring light to the new day.
Come to us in the birth
   of the infant Christ:
that we discover the fullness
   of your redemption
throughout the universe;
Mother and Child of Peace,
bound by the Spirit of Love,
One-in-Three forever. Amen.

DIVINE SEAMSTRESS

💕   Divine Seamstress,
we are the garment

You have stitched with love
to clothe your Holy Child.
We are the swaddling cloth
and the robe of one piece
torn by the failure of human compassion.
Enable us by your presence within us
to show forth the hope of Christ:
that suffering and oppression end,
and the hearts of people everywhere
beat with the fullness of your joy.
To You be praise,
Great Mother,
Vulnerable Child,
Spirit of Love,
One Divinity now and forever. Amen.

Christmas 1

GRANDMOTHER

- "There was a prophetess ... Anna ... now eighty-four years old.
  ... She came up just at [the moment Simeon blessed the child
  Jesus in the Temple] and began to praise God; and she spoke
  of the child to all who looked forward to the deliverance of
  Jerusalem." (Luke 2:36–38, NJB)

Grandmother,
your eyes of love shone
in the face of the prophetess Anna
as she welcomed the Christ Child to earth.
Draw us to You in the loving looks
    of our mothers and sisters:
that, supported by their tenderness,
we embody your radiance to others;

Wise Woman,
Maiden,
and Spirit of Innocence,
Divine One-in-Three forever. Amen.

Alternative Prayer for Christmas 1 based on John 1:1–18:
"The Feminine Divine as Homemaker" (p. 52).

Christmas 2

MOTHER OF THE UNIVERSE

- "Blessed be the God...who...chose us in Christ before the
  foundation of the world." (Ephesians 1:3–4, NRSV)

  Mother of the Universe,
    even before we were conceived
    You knew us by name
    as your daughters and sons.
    Cradle us in your goodness
       and love:
    that, binding creation to yourself,
    all humanity discover the joy
       of wholeness in You.
    Giver of Life,
    Holy Child,
    and Divine Love,
    You are Three-in-One,
    now and forever. Amen.

Alternative Prayer for Christmas 2 based on John 1:1–18:
"The Feminine Divine as Homemaker" (p. 52).

The Season of Epiphany

———— ✎ ————

IN EPIPHANY we know the feminine Divine as NURTURING
MOTHER, the One who puts us to the breast and feeds us,[1]
the One who sees that all our needs are met. In this season
we have the opportunity to experience ourselves once more
as small children and to receive the nurturing and discipline
that we may have missed when we were young.

We also experience Her as CHALLENGING MOTHER, the One
who weans us and disciplines us, gently pushing us toward responsible action for ourselves and preparing us for
a constructive role in community.

She is the One Who Draws Us into Mission and the One Who
Heals the Dis-ease of the World.

Always present throughout the cycle of the feminine Divine
is the GRANDMOTHER, THE AGING ONE who represents the

---

1. Mollenkott, *The Divine Feminine,* discusses the tradition of the Divine as
nursing Mother relating particularly to Jesus as One who feeds and nurtures (20–
25). She cites F. Cross in *Canaanite Myth and Hebrew Epic* in translating "Shaddai,"
the name given to God by Naomi in the Book of Ruth, as "the God with breasts,"
although most translations read "the Almighty" or "the Lord" (57–59). See Numbers
11:10–13: "Moses said to the Lord, . . . Did I conceive all this people? Did I bring them
forth, that thou shouldst say to me 'Carry them in your bosom, as a nurse carries
the sucking child, to the land which thou didst swear to give their fathers? . . . The
burden is too heavy for me. . . .' " (RSV).

movement of humanity toward death. This presence is loving and wise, but also embodies the mortality that we all share.

In this respect we experience Womangod as DEEP WINTER, frozen and "dead" earth, loss of warmth, extreme cold, the One who beckons us toward the end of our days. She is the deep snow of ensnarement yet beauty, life-threatening cold, storm and blizzard, or in milder climates She is heavy clouds, driving rain, or raging sea. At the same time She is the warm grandmother who draws us to sit near the fire and nourishes us with her loving understanding.

Thus the Trinity is present throughout: Grandmother, Mother, and Child (Christ, and the Child in each of us).

This feminine trinity far predates the masculine trinity of Father, Son, and Holy Spirit and is the shadow side of the trinity named in the time of patriarchy.

General Prayer

MOTHER EAGLE

- " . . . in the shadow of your wings I sing for joy." (Psalm 63:7, NRSV)

- "As an eagle stirred up her nest, fluttereth over her young, spreadeth abroad her wings, taketh them, beareth them upon her wings, so the Lord alone did lead Jacob." (Deuteronomy 32:11–12, KJV)

- "And Jesus said to them, 'Follow me and I will make you fish for people.' And immediately they left their nets and followed him." (Mark 1:17–18, NRSV)

୨୭ Mother Eagle,[2]
out of the dream of innocence
You wake us up.
When the time is right,
gently release us
from the shadow of your wings,
and nudge us from the nest:
that, responding to your call,
we carry your Word of justice
to every creature and nation.
We pray in the name of the Child Jesus.
Amen.

The Feast of the Epiphany

MOTHER HEN

- "[Jesus said,] 'Jerusalem, Jerusalem, you that kill the prophets
and stone those who are sent to you! How often have I longed to
gather your children together, as a hen gathers her brood under
her wings, and you refused!' " (Luke 13:34, NJB)

୨୭ Mother Hen,[3]
You watch over your chicks by day
and cover them with your wings by night.
Gather your children to the warmth of your breast:
that your church be strengthened by your care,
and in love reach out to embrace the world;
Mother, Child, and Spirit of Love,
now and everyday. Amen.

2. For a description of the image of the Divine as Eagle, see Mollenkott, *The Divine Feminine*, 83–91.
3. For a description of the image of the Divine as Mother Hen, see Mollenkott, *The Divine Feminine*, 92–96.

Epiphany 1 (Proper 1)

MOTHER OF CREATION

- Paul writes, "I... have been entrusted with... proclaiming...
  the unfathomable treasure of Christ and of throwing light on
  the inner workings of the mystery kept hidden through all the
  ages." (Ephesians 3:8–9, NJB)
- John the Baptist: "I have baptised you with water, but [Christ]
  will baptise you with the Holy Spirit." (Mark 1:8, NJB)

ॐ   Mother of Creation,
    in baptism your womb-waters break
       as we are born into new relationship
       with You and your community of faith.
    Flood us with the knowledge of your
       mercy and peace:
    that your church, embodying your healing
       presence throughout the world,
    encourage all humanity into friendship with You;
    Source of Life, Healing, and Justice,
       Divine One forever and ever. Amen.

Epiphany 2 (Proper 2)

ONE WHO CALLS IN THE NIGHT

- "I muse on you in the watches of the night...; in the shadow
  of your wings I rejoice." (Psalm 63:6–7, NJB)
- "...he counts out the number of the stars, and gives each one
  of them a name." (Psalm 147:4, NJB)
- "Yahweh then came and stood by, calling as he had done before,
  'Samuel! Samuel!' Samuel answered, 'Speak, Yahweh; for your
  servant is listening.'" (1 Samuel 3:10, NJB)

≫ One Who Calls in the Night,
   like the stars You have set in the heavens,
   You have created us for yourself
       and speak to us by name.
   Teach us to hear your voice
    even when we cannot see your face:
   that our hearts and minds be illumined
   by the knowledge of your steadfast love,
   and our lives proclaim with praise
       your presence in all the world;
   Inhabiter of Darkness,
   Bringer of Light,
   Numinous One. Amen.

Epiphany 3 (Proper 3)

WOMANGOD OUR ROCK AND SPRING

- "He alone is my rock and my salvation....I shall not be shaken." (Psalm 62:6, RSV)
- "Lord, you are my lover, my longing, my flowing stream." (Mechtild of Magdeburg[4])

≫ Womangod Our Rock and Spring,
   your strength is like the constancy
       of mountain slopes.
   Yet the flow of your mercy
   carves channels in the very foundations
   of our knowledge of You,
   and changes your shape.
   Sculpt our lives and the life of your church

---

4. Mechtild of Magdeburg, "How the Soul Speaks to God," in *Beguine Spirituality: An Anthology,* ed. Fiona Bowie (London: SPCK, 1989), 55.

by the movement of your steadfast love:
that, repenting of our failure to care
    for one other,
we become conduits of your compassion
    for all the world;
Nurturing Mother,
One Who Challenges Us,
Spirit of Wisdom. Amen.

Alternative Prayer for Epiphany 3 based on theme compatible
with Mark 1:14–20: "Mother Eagle" (Challenging Mother,
p. 56).

Epiphany 4 (Proper 4)

ROOT OF WISDOM

- "The root of wisdom is fear of Yahweh." (Psalm 111:10, NJB)
- "I will raise up for them a prophet ...; I will put my words in
  the mouth of the prophet, who shall speak to them everything
  that I command." (Deuteronomy 18:18, NRSV)
- "They were astounded at [Jesus'] teaching, for he taught them
  as one having authority, and not as the scribes." (Mark 1:22,
  NRSV)

    Root of Wisdom,
      from whom light and understanding sprout,
      You ground us in the warm soil
        of your discipline and love.
      Expand throughout all that is hidden
      from your grace:
      that, by your healing touch,
      all things become transformed
      and joy flourish in every human heart;

Mother of All,
Child of the New Dawn,
Heavenly Dove.
Amen.

Epiphany 5 (Proper 5)

Weaver of the Web of Life

- "I am allotted months of emptiness, and nights of misery. . . . My days are swifter than a weaver's shuttle." (Job 7:3, 6, NRSV)

- "Praise Yahweh! . . . He gathers together the exiles of Israel, healing the broken-hearted and binding up their wounds." (Psalm 147:1–4, NJB)

- "Now Simon's mother-in-law was . . . feverish. . . . [Jesus] . . . took her by the hand and helped her up. And the fever left her." (Mark 1:30–34, NJB)

✌ Weaver of the Web of Life,
with nimble fingers You sew our joys
and sorrows
into the tapestry of your creation,
and not a thread escapes your hand.
Hear the wail of the outcast ones
within us,
the brokenhearted, the downtrodden,
and the hungry:
that, knowing your motherly-compassion,
we hear the cries of others,
and minister in your Name
to all who are in need;
Creatress, Redemptress, and Sustainer,
Divine One-in-Three now and forever. Amen.

Epiphany 6

HEARER OF THE SLAVE GIRL

- "Naaman... suffered from a virulent skin-disease. Now, on one of their raids into Israelite territory, the Aramaeans had carried off a little girl, who became a servant of Naaman's wife. She said to her mistress, 'If only my master would approach the prophet of Samaria! He would cure him of his skin-disease.'" (2 Kings 5:1–14, NJB)

- "A man suffering from a virulent skin-disease came to him and pleaded... saying, 'If you are willing, you can cleanse me.'... Jesus... said to him, 'I am willing.'" (Mark 1:40, NJB)

     ☞   You with Healing in Your Wings,
          through the wisdom and caring of a slave girl,
          enabled Elisha to heal Naaman.
          Assist us by the power of your Holy Spirit
          to seek health for all those who are ill
              and in distress:
          that suffering be overcome,
          and all that is amiss in this universe
              be repaired;
          Wise Grandmother,
          Compassionate Child,
          Restoring Spirit. Amen.

Epiphany 7

SHEKINAH, DIVINE HEALING WOMAN, AND GRANDMOTHER OF THE OPPRESSED

"Shekinah": *See* Pentecost, Proper 9, p. 98.

- "Jesus took with him Peter and James and John and led them up a high mountain... in their presence he was transfigured...."

And a cloud came, covering them in shadow; and from the cloud there came a voice, 'This is my Son, the Beloved. Listen to him.' " (Mark 9:1–7, NJB)

"Divine Healing Woman": *See* Easter 7, p. 92.

- "Look, I am doing something new, now it emerges; can you not see it?" (Isaiah 43:19a, NJB)
- "Jesus said to the paralytic, 'My child, your sins are forgiven.' ... 'I order you: get up, pick up your stretcher, and go off home.' And the man got up ... and walked out in front of everyone." (Mark 2:5–12, NJB)

"Grandmother of the Oppressed": *See* Pentecost, Proper 22, p. 110, or "Heart of Compassion": *See* Pentecost, Proper 26, p. 113.

- " ... you shall love your neighbor as yourself." (Leviticus 19:18, NRSV)
- " ... love your enemies and pray for those who persecute you. ... You must therefore set no bounds to your love, just as your heavenly Father sets none to his." (Matthew 5:44, 48, NJB)

Epiphany 8

MOTHER OF ORPHANS

- "Blessed is anyone who cares for the poor and the weak." (Psalm 41:1, NJB)

    Mother of Orphans,
from deep within your belly
You pour out steadfast love
to redeem the vulnerable ones of the world.
The warmth of your eyes radiates strength,
and your touch is gentle and reassuring.

Speak to each of us
at our own points of woundedness:
that compassion stir within us
and issue in acts of justice and truth;
Wise Woman,
Crucified One,
Bearer of Justice. Amen.

ONE WHOSE LOVE IS ENOUGH

- "I was given a thorn in the flesh. . . . I have three times pleaded
  with the Lord that it might leave me; but he has answered me,
  'My grace is enough for you: for power is at full stretch in
  weakness.'" (2 Corinthians 12:7–9, NJB)

    One Whose Love Is Enough
and all that we can desire,
your power is made perfect
    in our vulnerability.
Continue to call us back to You
and to one another:
that, acknowledging You as the source
    of our strength and hope,
we claim the reality of your reign on earth.
Womangod,
emanating love, power, and justice,
You are our Goddess Three-in-One. Amen.

The Season of Lent

—— ❧ ——

I N LENT we know the feminine Divine as the MOTHER WHO LETS US GO and SHADOW SISTER. In Lent we experience Her in themes of puberty and adolescence. Although She is protective, She is also the Mother who pushes us toward taking responsibility for ourselves and claiming our freedom.

In puberty, as we turn to a new phase of life, She is source of anxiety and confusion, of disillusionment and loss of innocence. She is WILDERNESS as we discover and delve into our nonrational selves. We experience Her as Judge, Superego, Driving Spirit... but She is also the Promise of Freedom, the Listener, and the One who supports us in our effort to get free. We know Her in the support and common struggle of our sisters and brothers in the Way. She is the One who calls us to coming of age.

The passage from Lent to Easter involves recognition of our own oppression and the way women are objectified as inferior and as connected with evil. In Lent we learn to say no: no to the negative images of Mother given us in patriarchy, no to the pressure to conform to masculine models of success, no to the myth that we are dependent upon male protection (or possession) for safety and salvation, and no to the dominance of rational and masculine values. Sorting out fact from fiction is our wilderness experience, our quest for truth. As we search for our own souls, we discern Womangod in the prefigure of Christ as SHADOW SISTER.

In Lent, She Who Is[1] is the divine presence within all that is, and the inward movement that has enabled knowledge of ourselves and others and of life as human-divine encounter. She is the Lure that persuades us to let go of childhood self-indulgence and achieve passage into adult womanhood or manhood. She Who Is encourages us to let go of our acquiescence to oppression and reach out for freedom, empowerment, and a vision of wholeness in the context of mutuality and community.

In creation we experience Her as LATE WINTER and PREMONITION OF SPRING. We experience Her negatively like the bleakness of "dead" trees and the snow that darkens prior to the thaw.... Yet, She is the LENGTHENING OF DAYS as we see the promise of spring in the reddening wood of deciduous branches or in the saltiness of the morning air.

General Prayer

PREGNANT MOTHER

- "But whenever you give alms, do not let your left hand know what your right hand is doing, so that your alms may be done in secret.... But when you fast, put oil on your head and wash your face, so that your fasting may be seen... by your Father who is in secret." (Matthew 6:3, 17, NRSV)

- Pregnant Mother,
  in the darkness of your secret chamber

---

1. The title "She Who Is" is drawn from Elizabeth A. Johnson, *She Who Is: The Mystery of God in Feminist Theological Discourse* (New York: Crossroad, 1992).

your seeds of love sprout
and begin to seek the light.
Enable us to value the fertility
    of darkness in others:
that, accepting our sorrows and struggles,
we share the treasures
of your germinating power
    throughout the world;
God and Goddess in divine embrace,[2]
One in the Spirit forever. Amen.

Ash Wednesday

Divine Midwife

- "...the Day of Yahweh is coming...the earth quakes, the skies tremble, sun and moon grow dark, the stars lose their brilliance.... When that Day comes, the mountains will run with new wine and the hills will flow with milk, and all the stream-beds of Judah will run with water." (Joel 2:1, 10; 4:18, NJB)

❧   Divine Midwife,
    You are with us.
    Though the earth struggle and heave,
    and the sun and moon fail,
    You bring your people to birth.
    Help us to know the depth
        of your compassion:
    that, when this hour is over,
    we and all creation be moved
        by your Spirit

---

2. See Rafael Patai, *The Hebrew Goddess* (New York: KTAV, 1967), on this image of the Cherubim.

to join with Christ and live with You
in Glory, forever.
Amen.

Lent 1

WOMANGOD AS FLOOD (ONE WHO WEEPS FOR US)

- "I establish my covenant with you, that never again shall all
  flesh be cut off by the waters of a flood, and never again shall
  there be a flood to destroy the earth." (Genesis 9:11, NRSV)

❧   One Who Weeps for Us,
       in the midst of your pain
       You flood the earth
          with your life's blood,
       washing away all that distracts us
       from You and one another.
       Clarify to us the meaning of our baptism:
       that, when the waters recede,
       we will be cleansed and empowered
       by the tears of your compassion;
       Sorrowful Mother, Divine Child,
       Spirit of Mercy. Amen.

WOMANGOD AS RAINBOW

- "When I bring clouds over the earth and the bow is seen in the
  clouds, I will remember my covenant that is between me and
  you and every living creature." (Genesis 9:14–15, NRSV)

❧   Goddess of All Delight,
       You lead us into the rainbow of your Self.
       Let us bathe in the moisture of your healing

and bask in the warmth of your rosiness:
that we become witnesses of your faithfulness.
For You wrap the earth with your goodness
   and caress her with steadfast love;
Mother, Sister of our Hearts, One Divinity,
together with the Spirit of Wisdom. Amen.

WOMANGOD AS WILDERNESS

- " . . . the Spirit drove him into the desert and he remained there for forty days." (Mark 1:12, NJB)

One Who Dwells in Desert Places,
You are the Wilderness
   into whom we swarm,
seeking to ferret You out.
Continue to elude us:
that we search for You more deeply,
and come to maturity in the finding;
Goddess of Wind and Sand and Fire,
One Who Blossoms at the dew drop's touch.
Amen.

Lent 2

MOTHER OF SARAH AND ALL HUMANITY

- "God said to Abraham, 'As for Sarai your wife . . . I will bless her, and . . . she shall be a mother of nations.' . . . Then Abraham . . . laughed, and said to himself, ' . . . Shall Sarah, who is ninety years old, bear a child?' " (Genesis 17:15–19, RSV)
- "He [Abraham] . . . did not weaken in faith when he considered his own body . . . or . . . the barrenness of Sarah's womb." (Romans 4:19–25, RSV)

❧   Mother of All,
      when we feel that life has passed us by
      and imagine You no longer hear or care,
      You remind us of Sarah, survivor
          in a barren land,
      who discovered in old age that your grace
      creates justice beyond expectation.
      Calm the frantic churning of our hearts
          and minds,
      and turn us from attempts to save ourselves
          apart from your will:
      that we discover trust in the process
          You have begun in us,
      and dream dreams of that hope-beyond-hope
      given to all humanity in Jesus Christ,
      our Friend and our Redeemer. Amen

Alternative Prayer for Lent 2 based on Mark 8:31–38: "Kernel of Grain" (p. 73).

Alternative Prayer for Lent 2 based on Mark 9:2–8: "Shekinah" (p. 98).

Lent 3

MOTHER WISDOM

- The giving of the Law. (Exodus 20:1–17)
- "The Law of Yahweh is ... wisdom for the simple." (Psalm 19:7, NJB)
- "Wisdom calls aloud in the streets, she raises her voice in the public squares.... 'Pay attention to my warning. To you I will pour out my heart and tell you what I have to say.' " (Proverbs 1:20, 23, NJB)

🐛   Mother Wisdom[3]
You cry for justice at the street corners,[4]
and pour out your heart to any who will listen.
Implant the spirit of your law of love within us:
that, turning aside from greed and wrongdoing,
we be wrapped in the cloak of your saving judgment
and adorned with the jewels of your intelligence.
Womangod,
You are the One Who Watches over Us,
our Passionate Friend,
and the Spirit of Truth. Amen.

Lent 4

PERSISTENT LOVER

- Despite the unfaithfulness of priests and people, "The Lord...
  sent persistently to them by his messengers, because he had compassion on his people...; but they kept mocking the messengers
  of God." (2 Chronicles 36:15–16, NRSV)

- "For God so loved the world that he gave his only Son, so that
  everyone who believes in him may not perish but may have
  eternal life." (John 3:16, NRSV)

🐛   Most Beloved in heaven and earth,
You come to us like a persistent lover,
longing to be received.
No sacrifice is too much for You.
Awake in us the stirrings of hope:
that, trusting in the goodness of your ardor,
we come into the fullness of union with You;

---

3. Title suggested by Jean Horton.
4. Mollenkott, *The Divine Feminine,* 98.

Mother, Sister, and Child,
She Who Is for all eternity. Amen.

STORM-GODDESS

- The king of the Chaldeans attacked Jerusalem, killing everyone, burning the Temple and palaces to the ground, and destroying the walls of the city. (2 Chronicles 36:17–19)

    Storm-Goddess,
    when the devastations of our lives
    threaten to overturn us,
    we imagine your anger in the thunder
      and the lashing of the wind.
    Yet in the pounding of the rain
    we discover your tears
    and know that humans alone have brewed
      this storm.
    Show us the destructiveness
      of our hearts and minds,
    and bring home to us the consequences
      of our own actions:
    that, seeking to make amends
      to a ravaged world,
    we work for peace among all peoples;
    Goddess in Terror,
    Goddess in Calm,
    Goddess All-in-all.
    Amen.

Lent 5

KERNEL OF GRAIN

- " ... truly, I tell you, unless a grain of wheat falls into the earth and dies, it remains just a single grain; but if it dies, it bears much fruit." (John 12:24, NRSV)

> Kernel of Grain
> You are the seed snuggling within us,
> sleeping until it is time to wake
>   and stretch.
> Thread your roots into the earthworks
>   of our souls and bodies:
> that, by your warming, moistening power,
> the soft tissue of your presence spread
>   throughout the church,
> and burst forth with beauty
>   in the garden of New Creation;
> Planter, Nurturer,
> and Enlivener of all that is
>   and will be forever,
> world without end. Amen.

COMPANION IN THE LONGEST NIGHT

- "Now my soul is troubled. And what should I say — 'Father, save me from this hour'?" (John 12:27, NRSV)
- "Jesus offered up prayers ... with loud cries and tears. ... he learned obedience through what he suffered." (Hebrews 5:7–8, NRSV)
- "Create in me a clean heart, O God, and put a new and right spirit within me." (Psalm 51:10, NRSV)

❧   Companion in the Longest Night,
      in Christ's acceptance of death on the cross,
      You call us to let go of our defenses
      and face the pain and death in our own lives.
      Open our hearts and minds to the knowledge
      that in our suffering You suffer,
      and in your suffering our pain is given meaning:
      that, releasing all that locks in pain and death,
      we are freed to embrace a new dimension
          of your grace and healing;
      Sorrowful Mother, Crucified One, Breath of Life.
      Amen.

Holy Week

— ❧ —

I N HOLY WEEK we experience the feminine Divine as death of adolescence and the death of our illusions about ourselves. The adolescent dies and the adult is ready to be born. The woman or man sees through the false myths of patriarchy and moves to get free. There is a terrible wrenching in the letting go of parental authority, accepting our own responsibility for our lives, and gathering the strength to push free. Holy Week involves this dying and the time of gathering strength. It is at once a return to the womb and a cutting of the umbilical cord, the lifeline of dependency. Holy Week enables us to move from the passivity of a kind of emotional osmosis in the climate of our biological or adopted family and in patriarchy, to conscious choices within the mutuality and support that make mature life possible.

In Holy Week, Womangod is known as SORROWFUL MOTHER, the One who lets us go and who suffers our pain. She is also known as our WOUNDED SISTER, for there is no moving to freedom without a wound. As Wounded Sister, She shows us the way through the impasse of our attachment to parental authority and patriarchy that hold us back from breaking free and becoming persons in our own right. She assists us in the move to intimacy with others outside our families of origin and to a community based on values of freedom and equality.

At this time She moves in our Budding Sexuality, which involves both wound and the possibility of joy.

She is again the PREGNANT MOTHER, containing us emotionally as we prepare to move to birth in a new phase of life. In the women who support Jesus through anointing him, remaining awake at Gethsemane, and standing with him at the foot of the cross, She is MIDWIFE as we seek to make the passage from adolescence into adulthood — essentially giving birth to ourselves in and through her creative Spirit.

(Note: Prayers in this section are for the most part thematic rather than based on the lectionary.)

Passion Sunday

WOUNDED ONE

- "Then Jesus gave a loud cry, and breathed his last. And the curtain of the temple was torn in two, from top to bottom." (Mark 15:37–38, NRSV)

     Wounded One,
       we see You in all those who suffer violence
         at the hands of the strong and powerful:
       women and children battered and raped,
       young men conscripted against their wills,
       and whole peoples starved in acts of genocide.
       As You in your death on the cross join
         in human suffering,
       enable us to give up our lives of privilege
       and stand with the poor and the powerless:
       that the joy of your redemption be not long
       in coming to a world desperate for your compassion.

We pray to You, Sorrowful Mother,
Passionate Savior,
Spirit of Love. Amen.

Holy Monday

MOTHER OF ALL

- "Seeing a fig tree in leaf some distance away, [Jesus] went to see if he could find any fruit on it, but . . . he found nothing but leaves; for it was not the season for figs." (Mark 11:12–14, NJB) This story of the cursing of the fig tree seems unworthy of the Jesus of love and justice; however, in the context of holy week we are reminded of the myth of Demeter, who, when her daughter Persephone was raped and carried off to the underworld, in her grief withheld the greening of the earth.

☙ Mother of All,
    when your children are violated
      and carried away,
    your Spirit suffers:
    the waters of the earth dry up,
    the trees withhold their fruits,
    and all the earth groans
    with the pain of hunger.
    Return from their prisons all who are lost,
    and restore the lives of those whose faith
      has died:
    that, in due season, we harvest once more
      all that we need,
    and sing and shout and dance for joy
    at the coming of your Glory;
    Sorrowful Mother,
    Wounded Sister,

Transforming Spirit,
Triune Goddess for all times. Amen.

Holy Tuesday

SHADOW SISTER IN THE UNKNOWN WOMAN
WHO ANOINTED JESUS

- " ... two days before the Passover ... a woman came with an alabaster jar of very costly ointment of nard, and she ... poured the ointment on [Jesus'] head. ... Jesus said, 'Let her alone; why do you trouble her? ... she has anointed my body ... for its burial. Truly I tell you, wherever the good news is proclaimed in the whole world, what she has done will be told in remembrance of her.' " (Mark 14:1, 3–9, NRSV).

❧ Passionate Sister,
when Jesus' disciples were full of doubt
and on the verge of flight,
You came to him in the love of the woman
who anointed his head with costly oil.
Keep in us the memory of her:[1] that, whenever the
work that we do
is opposed or trivialized,
we are strengthened by her boldness and trust
and restored to the fragrance of your love;
Companion in Life, Death, and Resurrection:
Womanchrist. Amen.

---

1. For reflection on this story, see Elisabeth Schüssler Fiorenza, *In Memory of Her: A Feminist Theological Reconstruction of Christian Origins* (New York: Crossroad, 1984), xiii–xiv; and M. Procter-Smith, *In Her Own Rite: Constructing Feminist Liturgical Tradition* (Nashville: Abingdon Press, 1990), 36–58.

Holy Wednesday

WOMANGOD AS STREAM

- " ... anyone who trusts in Yahweh ... is like a tree by the waterside that thrusts its roots to the stream: when the heat comes it has nothing to fear, its foliage stays green; untroubled in a year of drought, it never stops bearing fruit." (Jeremiah 17:7–8, NJB)

☙ Sourcewater[2] of Life,
You are the stream
into which we thrust our roots.
Running beside us,
You quench our thirst forever.
Neither the heat of the noonday sun
nor the cold of the desert night
can bring us to harm.
Well up in us from the center of the earth:
that, trusting in your replenishing love,
we give away all that we have
and all that we are to those in need;
Ocean of All Wisdom,
Spring of Our Desire,
Baptizing Spirit,
Womangod, now and forever. Amen.

Alternative Prayer for Holy Wednesday based on John 12:27–36 by comparing Demeter and the Owner of the Vineyard whose son was murdered: *see* Holy Monday, "Mother of All," (p. 77).

---

2. The image of "Sourcewater" or "Womanwater" is drawn from a meditation by Diane Mariechild, *Mother Wit: A Feminist Guide to Psychic Development* (Trumansburg, N.Y.: Crossing Press, 1981), 13.

Maundy Thursday

HOLY FOUNTAIN

- "Moses ... sprinkled [the blood] over the people, saying, 'This is the blood of the covenant which Yahweh has made with you.'" (Exodus 24:8, NJB)
- "The blessing-cup which we bless, is it not a sharing in the blood of Christ?" (1 Corinthians 10:16–17, NJB)

❧ Holy Fountain, Source of All Goodness,
You flow within us with power and purpose,
and in the shedding of blood offer a sign
of hope to the world.
Inundate us with the exuberance of Christ's love
poured out for us:
that the life which You have formed in your church
flood into acts of justice, mercy, and compassion;
Life-giving Blood,
Sustaining Bread,
mingled with Love.
Amen.

THE WOMEN UNNAMED AT THE LORD'S SUPPER

- Observance of the absence of the naming of women present at the Last Supper.

❧ Shadow Sister,
before we knew You,
You were present at the Last Supper
in the women who followed Jesus,
hungering for Wisdom.
Be present in us today as we reenact this meal:
that the intimacy shared with Christ that night

be available to all who seek to know You this night;
Thou, Wise Mother,
Vulnerable One,
Beckoning Spirit,
Womangod One-in-Three. Amen.

Good Friday

The Goddess in the Women Who Did Not Flee[3]

- "All of [the disciples] deserted [Jesus] and fled." (Mark 14:50, nrsv)

- "At that moment the cock crowed for the second time. Then Peter remembered that Jesus had said to him, 'Before the cock crows twice, you will deny me three times.' And he broke down and wept." (Mark 14:72, nrsv)

- "There were also women looking on from a distance.... These used to follow [Jesus] and provided for him... in Galilee; and there were many other women who had come up with him to Jerusalem." (Mark 15:40–41, nrsv)

   Womangod,
     when one betrayed and many fled,
     You remained with Jesus
     in the women who did not desert him,
     and who, witnessing his crucifixion,
     suffered their hearts to be pierced.
     Keep in our memory these faithful disciples:
     that, following in their example,
     we share the pain of all who suffer;
     Sorrowful Woman,

---

3. Elisabeth Moltmann Wendel, *The Women Around Jesus* (London: SCM Press, 1982), 107–13, discusses how the male disciples of Jesus fled in disarray from the garden of Gethsemane, while the women remained steadfast throughout the Passion of Christ.

Vulnerable One,
Holy Comforter. Amen.

Holy Saturday

WOMEN AT THE BURIAL OF JESUS

- "[Pilate]...granted the corpse to Joseph who...took Jesus
  down from the cross...and laid him in a tomb....Mary of
  Magdala and Mary the mother of Joset took note of where he
  was laid." (Mark 15:45–47, NJB; see also Matthew 27:57–61)

> Sorrowful Mother,
> in the hearts and eyes of the two Marys
> You watched where the body of your Child
>   was laid to rest,
> and You wept.
> Show us how to grieve
> for the lost and forsaken ones:
> that, facing the reality of your pain,
> we renew our journey with You
> in the redemption of the world;
> Womb of Humanity,
> Crucified One,
> and Birth-giving Spirit,
> One Divinity now and forever. Amen.

The Season of Easter

———— ❧ ————

I N EASTER we celebrate the completion of our passage from childhood into maturity and from oppression into empowerment. We have moved through the death of former perceptions and ways of being into new life and a new community. We have experienced conversion from patriarchy and welcome the promise of wholeness in the Easter community.

In Easter we identify and receive our power, accepting the image of Womangod within us. By receiving Her into ourselves, we give up the myth of passive dependence on others and move into the Way of mutuality and wholeness as part of the Body of Christ.

In Easter, if we have received the nurture and strengthening we need, we move beyond preoccupation with ourselves into community where we form strong, adult friendships. As the Risen Christ appeared not only to individuals but to whole communities in which each of us sees our Self in the other, we recognize that the feminine Divine outside of us, beyond our experience, is also the Goddess within us, empowering us to a new way of seeing the world and of living together. In Easter She becomes SOUL SISTER and ALLURING WISDOM. As RISEN WOMAN She becomes for us the WOMANCHRIST.

We celebrate Easter in the imagery of spring: budding, green-ing, radiance, the crocus that breaks through the snow, the daffodil that pushes through the soil, the cherry tree that bursts into blossom.... We celebrate also with images of the New Woman, of New Humanity, and of the New Creation.

General Prayer

EARTH DANCER

- The Cree word for "peace" — *chiyamayitamowin* — is "a de-scription of the moment in the spring when after a rain, all is fresh and green as the sun emerges...as though...all of cre-ation is gathering its forces to surge forward to grow, blossom and push toward fruition with the single focus of becoming all it was meant to be." (Caleb Lawrence)[1]

    Earth Dancer,
    on this day of days
    You change your clothes of mourning
    for a robe of rejoicing.
    Your skirts, green as the spring grass,
    sparkle with dew drops in the rising sun,
    and blossoms of morning-glory
    spill from your apron as You swirl.
    Erase from us the fear of death
      in all its forms:
    that, opening to new life,
    we bloom and grow in the warmth
      of your love;
    Mother of All,

1. Caleb Lawrence, in Joyce Carlson, ed., *Journey: Stories and Prayers for the Christian Year from the People of the First Nations* (Toronto: Anglican Book Centre, 1991), 47.

Risen One,
Spirit of Joy.
Amen.

Easter Vigil

SISTER WHO JOURNEYS WITH US

❧ Sister Who Journeys with Us,
You die with the ebb of life
and rise with the flow,
and You help us to break through
the cocoons of our childhood wounds.
Open our eyes to the wonder of your love:
that we experience the trust
that has eluded us,
and discover a new level of friendship
with You and all humanity;
Embryo, Chrysalis, and Butterfly,
One Divinity in all seasons. Amen.

WOMAN OF TRANSFORMING POWER

- "Tremble, O earth, at the presence of the Lord...who turns the rock into a pool of water, the flint into a spring." (Psalm 114:7–8, NRSV)

- "Do you not know that all of us who have been baptized into Christ Jesus were baptized into his death? Therefore we have been buried with him...so that...as Christ was raised from the dead..., we too might walk in newness of life." (Romans 6:3–11, NRSV)

❧ Woman of Transforming Power,
in the midst of the wasteland

> You create an oasis
> where trees shelter us
> from the blazing sun.
> Invite us to drink of your living waters:
> that, leaving behind the places of death,
> we enter into the community
> whose promise is Shalom.
> Creative One,
> Soul Sister,
> Alluring Wisdom:
> You are Womanchrist.
> Amen.

See Also "Mother of Sarah and All Humanity," (p. 69), "Root of Wisdom" (p. 60), and "Mother Wisdom" (p. 70).

Easter Day

MARY MAGDALENE, FIRST APOSTLE[2]

- "Woman, why are you weeping?" ... "I have seen the Lord." (John 20:16, 18, NRSV)

> Mother of Orphans and the Dispossessed,
> by your grace new life springs from the jaws of death.
> In the vision of the Risen Christ
>> we know pain at the loss of the old order,
>> and terror at the intrusion of the new.
> Yet, as You restored Mary Magdalene to wholeness,
>> You have touched our lives with healing,

---

2. See Elisabeth Moltmann-Wendel, *The Women Around Jesus*, 61–90 for interpretation of the role of Mary Magdalene in the Easter narrative.

and we have shared the joy and fulfillment
of community with You and one another.
We have stood with You at the foot of the cross,
and followed your broken body to the tomb.
We have known your absence
and searched to find You again,
and in your Body the church
we meet you face to face.
Speak to us gently and give us the zeal to run
with your first apostle Mary,
to proclaim that grief is past
and the coming of your new creation assured:
that your justice prevail in the minds and hearts
of all persons,
and every division of heaven and earth
be made One in You;
through Jesus Christ our Redeemer,
in the power of the Holy Spirit,
world without end. Amen.

Brief version:

    ✨   Mother of Orphans and the Dispossessed,
in the vision of the risen Christ,
we discover the courage to let go of the old
and reach for new life.
Inspire us to run with your apostle Mary
to proclaim the sure success of your love and justice:
that every division of heaven and earth
be brought to wholeness,
through Jesus Christ our Redeemer. Amen.

WOMEN'S EXPERIENCE OF THE EMPTY TOMB

- "Do not be amazed; you seek Jesus of Nazareth, who was crucified. He has risen, he is not here.... Go, tell... and they said
  nothing to any one, for they were afraid." (Mark 16:1–8, RSV)

❧   Grandmother of the Two Marys and Salome,
      in the midst of our mourning,
      You surprise us with the joy of resurrection.
      Bring to birth in us
      the knowledge that Christ lives in us
          and in all humanity:
      that, healed of the fears that besiege us,
      we proclaim the good news of your justice,
          which reigns forever;
      Alleluia! Amen.

Easter 2

HEARTBEAT OF THIS EARTH

- "Now the whole group of those who believed were of one heart
  and soul, and no one claimed private ownership of any posses-
  sions, but everything they owned was held in common." (Acts
  4:32, NRSV)
- "Jesus came and stood among them and said, 'Peace be with
  you.'" (John 20:19, NRSV)

❧   Heartbeat[3] of this Earth,
      in the ebb and flow
          of your steadfast love
      You bring us into being

---

3. It has been suggested that the drums of North American aboriginal peoples
mark the sound of the heartbeat of the Divine (from a workshop led by Mary Jane
Wilson, Redemptorist Centre, Edmonton, Alberta, Canada).

and make us one flesh with You.
Throb within the breasts of all believers:
that your church become the pulse
of your body the universe,
and share in the process
of the redemption of all creation;
Lover, Beloved, and Love itself. Amen.

Easter 3

BAKERWOMAN

- "Then they told what had happened on the road [to Emmaus],
  and how [Jesus] had been made known to them in the breaking
  of the bread." (Luke 24:35–48, NRSV)

Bakerwoman,
   in the bread You have made for us
      with your own hands,
   and the wine You have poured out for us
      with your whole life,
You are forever present with and in us.
Stir up among us a vision of your Shalom
in which every person receives what is needed,
and each is given dignity in the eyes of all:
that those who possess wealth, power, and wisdom
share with the poor, the powerless, and the lost,
and hatred, envy, and strife disappear
   from the face of the earth;
Brooding Spirit, One Full of Grace, Earthy One.
Amen.

Easter 4

SHEPHERDESS OF THE UNIVERSE

- "The Lord is my Shepherd...." (Psalm 23)
- "I am the good shepherd." (John 10:11–18, NRSV)
- "While [Jacob] was still speaking with them, Rachel came with her father's sheep; for she kept them." (GENESIS 29:9, NRSV)
- "The priest of Midian had seven daughters. They came to draw water, and filled the troughs to water their father's flock." (Exodus 2:16–21, NRSV) Even today women and children herd sheep in many lands.
- "As [Jesus] went ashore, he saw a great crowd; and he had compassion for them, because they were like sheep without a shepherd; and he began to teach them many things." (Mark 6:34, NRSV)

> ❧   Shepherdess of the Universe,
>   like Zipporah and Rachel
>   You care for your flock
>   as for creatures of value,
>   and we graze on the hillside
>   of your steadfast love.
>   You watch over us and speak to us
>   with the voice of a Friend.
>   Do not leave us to our own confusion.
>   Rather, lead us to a vision of a community
>   where all receive what they need;
>   Nurturer, Protector, and Eye of Love. Amen.

Easter 5

GODDESS OF THE LEAFY VINE

- "I am the true vine, and my Father is the vinegrower." (John 15:1–8, NRSV)

❧ Goddess of the Leafy Vine,
You who sprout from the brown soil
of creation and are yet divine;
You who creep along the earth
and wind up tree trunks to see the sky;
You who flourish with greenness
and burst forth with ripe red fruit;
send your church into the world
as the fragile tendril of your love
longing to gain its foothold:
that all peoples become one with Christ
and dwell with joy as Easter people,
together with You and the Holy Spirit,
world without end. Amen.

Easter 6

Risen Sister

- "Sing a new song to Yahweh ... [who] has ... revealed his saving justice for the nations to see. . . . Let the sea thunder. . . . Let the rivers clap their hands." (Psalm 98:1–2, 4–8, NJB)
- "No one has greater love than this, to lay down one's life for one's friends." (John 15:13, NRSV)

❧ Risen Sister,
all the earth breaks into song
at your coming,
the seas roar and the rivers clap
their hands.
Where you were battered and wounded,
You are restored to health.
Where you were enslaved and used,

You are set free.
Awake in us the joy of knowing
that You have opened the path to freedom
    for all who are oppressed:
that, giving up the masks
    of our subservience,
we empower others to claim the humanity
to which You call each of us;
Liberating Goddess, Empowering Sister,
Spirit of Hope. Amen.

Easter 7

DIVINE HEALING WOMAN

- This prayer is set in opposition to the dualism expressed in
  the Johannine passage assigned for this day (John 17:11b–19)
  and the hierarchical view of priesthood in Exodus 28. Healing
  women in the Middle Ages found healing powers of the Divine within creation. They stood against the movement in their
  time away from divine benevolence seen in nature to doctrines
  of "pure spirit," which split us off from our bodies and our
  mandate to care for the earth.

    Divine Healing Woman,
    Earth-cherisher and knower of herbs
        from dark forests,
    your intuitive knowledge of our minds and bodies
        reveals where our dis-ease lies
        and what it is we need
        to be restored to well-being.
    Touch us with your compassion:
    that, freed from all that separates us
    from You, ourselves, and others,

> we come into the full bloom of health and justice
>> in your land of Shalom;
> Thou, Life-giving Spirit,
> true expression of the Creative Word. Amen.

Ascension of the Lord

BROODING SPIRIT

- "With all wisdom and insight he has made known to us the mystery of his will, according to his good pleasure that he set forth in Christ, as a plan for the fullness of time, to gather up all things in him, things in heaven and things on earth." (Ephesians 1:8–10, NRSV)

> Brooding Spirit,
> with holy fingers You fashion all that is,
> giving life and substance to formless void.
> In your wisdom knit together that which is divided,
> and so join heaven and earth, body and spirit,
> male and female, light and dark:
> that, freed of the fragmentation
> that impedes our coming to You,
> we are drawn toward the vision of your Glory
> in which justice is shared by all,
> and creation is made whole in You;
> You Who Are Three-in-one,
> True Divinity. Amen.

The Season of Pentecost

———— ❧ ————

I N PENTECOST we know the feminine Divine as the One who brings us, female and male, to fruitful participation in the creative process of the Universe. She moves us through the stages of adulthood. We know Her in the imagery of late spring and of summer — rampant blossoms, flowing rivers, warmth, and showers — and autumn — the brilliance of leaves before they fall, the musty smell of decay, the increasing bite of the air, and all of nature letting go.

She is the ENABLING ONE, the One who has brought us through the passage from adolescence into adulthood and from oppression into freedom. She shows us how to define our boundaries so that we are protected against exploitation. She empowers us to stand strong in the face of oppression. She gives us the courage to confront evil. Out of the fruitfulness of her justice-making, She helps us stretch to become justice-makers. Washbourn's developmental stage that matches early Pentecost is that of commitment in relationships and vocation, including young motherhood.

As OUR RIPENING, Womangod is the embodiment of the mature woman, the FRUITFUL ONE. Developmentally, She is the Matron, the Organizer and Overseer, both in terms of vocation and in the community. Competent in these spheres, She reaches beyond her immediate relationships to help others. The fruit She bears is justice for all and compassion for those in need. She becomes Redemptress of the Oppressed. Yet her authority is not exerted as "power-over" but is the empowerment of the Spirit by which She continues to nurture and support us and all creation.

As QUEEN OF THE UNIVERSE, Womangod moves from the role of personal Friend to that of wise and competent Overseer of not only our world but the whole universe. Her relationship with the universe is that of Lover and Friend. She becomes Wisdom personified. She is our Grandmother. This role does not assume that family and children are essential for every woman; it is the spiritual role of Wise Woman, the One who sees beyond the immediate situation to the issues of the heart.

Finally, Womangod is the ONE WHO BRINGS US HOME, like the river or stream that carries us to our destination. As we move to the time of harvest, She is the One who discerns good and evil and gives the gifts of healing. In harmony with the universe, She holds in her hand the powers of life and death. To Her, death is as normal as life and part of the life process. As the One who enables our passage through death into the next life She is the Priestess of Death and again the MIDWIFE of our final birthing through which we return to total love in the Womb of All.

DIVINE ENABLING ONE (PROPERS 9–13)

General Prayer

WOMANGOD AS RIVER

- "Look, I am doing something new, now it emerges; can you not
  see it?...rivers in wastelands...for my people, my chosen one,
  to drink." (Isaiah 43:18–20, NJB)

- Flowing River,
  water of fluidity and power,
  You carve the imprint of your Being
  into the earth-banks past which You surge.
  Sculpt our lives and the life of your church
  by the movement of your Spirit:
  that we draw from the brief span of our mortality
  the good that you long for us to know;
  through the begotten, crucified, and risen One.
  Amen.

Day of Pentecost

WOMANSPIRIT

- "...suddenly there came from heaven a sound as of a violent
  wind which filled the entire house.... They were all filled with
  the Holy Spirit." (Acts 2:1, NJB)

- "Dry bones, hear the word of Yahweh.... I am now going to
  make breath enter you, and you will live." (Ezekiel 37:4, NJB)

- Womanspirit,[1]
  You come to us on the Four Winds,

---

1. Title drawn from Carol P. Christ and Judith Plaskow, eds., *Womanspirit Rising*
(San Francisco: Harper & Row, 1979).

and, by the power of the resurrection,
breathe your Self into all flesh
and make dry bones to walk
and carry the weight of human life.
Create in us hearts of love:
that, empowered as agents of your
transforming purpose,
we share the grace of your mercy
throughout the world;
Woman of Night, Woman of Dawn,
Soul-Sister. Amen.

See also "BROODING SPIRIT" (p. 93). Ascension Day

Trinity Sunday

ONE WHO MAKES THE GROUND HOLY

- "Moses, Moses! ... Take off your sandals, for the place where you are standing is holy ground. I am the God of your ancestors." (Exodus 3:4, NJB)

Womangod,
You who make the ground holy,
You guided and fed our ancestors
with the flame that neither destroys
nor can be extinguished.
Catch us up in the vision of your power
to make all things new:
that we labor with You
in bringing this universe into its fullness;
Thou, Soil of our Rootedness,
Bread of Heaven,

Fiery Spirit,
Lady Three-in-One. Amen.

Proper 9 (May 29–June 4)

SHEKINAH[2]

- "It is God who said, 'Let light shine out of darkness,' ...to enlighten them with the knowledge of God's glory, the glory on the face of Christ." (2 Corinthians 4:6, NJB)

   Cloud of Radiance,
   You cover us with the shadow
     of your compassion,
   and cloak us in the circle
     of your love.
   Your very darkness becomes for us
     an illumination.
   Lead us in your paths of justice
     and truth:
   that, moistened with the waters
     of baptism,
   our way is lighted into your eternal Glory;
   Divine Wisdom, Vision of Mercy,
   Pillar of Fire, the One Triune Goddess.
   Amen.

---

2. The Shekinah, the numinous presence of God that surrounded the arc of the covenant and cloud that led the Israelites through the wilderness, was considered a feminine presence. See Patai, *The Hebrew Goddess*, 99–120.

Proper 10 (June 5–11)

AWAKENING DAWN

- " . . . in the shadow of your wings I take refuge. . . . Awake, my glory, awake, lyre and harp, that I may wake the Dawn."[3] (Psalm 57:1, 8, NJB)

    Dawn of Glory,
    You call us from the Shadow
    of your wings of night
    to sing and dance to the melodies
      of your love and faithfulness.
    Save us from the times of trouble:
    that, absorbing the wisdom
      of your compassion,
    we rise above all that would confuse
      and destroy us,
    and enter into the radiance
      of the Land of your Shalom;
    Woman of Night,
    Morning Star,
    Dew of Heaven. Amen.

Alternative Prayer for Pentecost Proper 10 based on 2 Corinthians 4:13–18: "Hidden Treasure" (p. 111).

- "So we do not lose heart . . . because we look not at what can be seen but at what cannot be seen; for what can be seen is temporary, but what cannot be seen is eternal." (2 Corinthians 4:16–18, NRSV)

---

3. The New Jerusalem Bible states that Wisdom in this passage is personified as Dawn (note 57b, 871).

Proper 11 (June 12–18)

MUSTARD SEED GODDESS

- "[God's reign] is like a mustard seed which, at the time of its sowing, is the smallest of all the seeds on earth. Yet ... it grows into the biggest shrub of them all." (Mark 4:30–34, NJB)

℘   Mustard Seed Goddess,
    like a tiny seed embedded in earth,
    You plant yourself into the flesh
       of our hearts.
    Shoot forth the dark green branches
       of your love within us,
    and brighten our interior spaces
    with the gold of myriad blossoms:
    that the pungency of your oils
    heal the spirit of the universe;
    Fruit-bearing Woman,
    Blossom of Life,
    Spirit of Wisdom. Amen.

Proper 12 (June 19–25)

WEAVER OF THE UNIVERSE

- "So for anyone who is in Christ, there is a new creation." (2 Corinthians 5:17, NJB)

℘   Weaver of the Universe,
    from the beauty of your vision
       of Shalom
    You spin seamless cloth
    luminous with your greening,
    and unfold the fabric

of a new heaven and earth.
Weave in us the threads
    of your passion for justice:
that, trusting in the knowledge
    of your resurrection,
we stand with courage
in the face of all evil;
One Who Encompasses All Things,
Creatress, Redemptress,
and Sustainer. Amen.

Alternative Prayer for Pentecost Proper 12 based on Mark 4:35–41: "Storm-Goddess" (p. 72) see Lent 4.

- "A great windstorm arose, and the waves beat into the boat, so that the boat was already being swamped.... [Jesus] woke up and rebuked the wind and said to the sea, 'Peace! Be still!' Then the wind ceased, and there was a dead calm." (Mark 4:37, 39, NRSV)

Proper 13 (June 26–July 2)

GODDESS OF THE CHERUBIM

- "David went...to bring up the ark of God, who bears the title 'Yahweh Sabaoth, enthroned on the winged creatures.' " (2 Samuel 6:2, NJB)

    Goddess of the Cherubim,
      You call us to be lovers
        of one another
      and to learn and grow
        from our differences.
      Fill us with your passion
      to give dignity and honor

to every creature on this planet:
that, united by the chemistry
of your ecstatic presence,
all humanity enter into the bliss
    of your embrace;
Enchantress, Love-Child,
Source of All Desire,
One Goddess, now and forever. Amen.

DIVINE HEALING WOMAN

- "My daughter, . . . your faith has restored you to health; go in peace." (Mark 5:21–43, NJB)

●   Divine Healing Woman,
        as your Child Jesus returned
        Jairus's daughter to life
        and broke the power
        of a woman's hemorrhage,
        You take away the wounds of the past
        and open a path to wellness
           for all creation.
        Touch us with the knowledge
        of your saving health:
        that the universe in all its parts
        come into unity with You;
        Creatress, Redemptress,
           and Spirit of Hope. Amen.

THE FEMININE DIVINE AS MATURE WOMAN (PROPERS 14–20)

General Prayers

GODDESS OUR RIPENING

❧ Goddess Our Ripening,
by your love you sweeten us
and bring us to maturity.
Make us ruddy with the glow
of your health within us:
that, plump with your nurture,
we are strengthened for the time of harvest;
Old Healing Woman,
Wise Matron,
and Dawn of Glory,
the Triune Goddess for all seasons.
Amen.

VINEYARD OF OUR DELIGHT

- "But look, I am going to . . . speak to her heart. There I shall give her back her vineyards." (Hosea 2:14–23, NJB)
- "I come into my garden, my sister, my promised bride, I pick my myrrh and balsam, I eat my honey and my honeycomb, I drink my wine and milk." (Song of Solomon 5:1, NJB)

❧ Vineyard of Our Delight,
your pungent juiciness entices us,
and the fragrance of rare plants
lures us into the lushness of your Being.
Shade us with branches laden with pomegranates.
Feed us with Christ our Vine,

and lead us to drink of the wellspring
  of your abundant love:
that we, who were driven from your garden
  and forbidden its fruits,
be restored into union with You and all creation;
Alleluia! Amen.

Proper 14 (July 3–9)

DEFENDER OF WOMEN AND CHILDREN

- "Is not this...the son of Mary?"[4] (Mark 6:1–6, NRSV)

ᔰ   Defender of Women and Children,
     out of the pain of rejection
     You molded Jesus' heart of compassion,
     and caused Him to rise up
     in behalf of outcasts and sinners.
     Open our hearts to the despised
     and rejected ones of the world:
     that, surrounding them
     with the intensity of your love,
     we bring them into your household
     to be cherished by You forever;
     Friend and Advocate of the Lost,
     Liberating One. Amen.

---

4. According to Stephen Mitchell in *The Gospel according to Jesus,* 19–28, Jesus'
position as son of Mary rather than son of Joseph suggests that Jesus was perceived
as illegitimate and suffered with Mary the rejection normal to that society. One
could conclude that his compassion for women and love of children stems from this
experience of rejection. See the discussion on p. 24 above.

Proper 15 (July 10–16)

INTIMATE FRIEND

- "Father" as an expression of intimacy rather than authority. (Ephesians 1:3)
- Jesus "ordered them to take nothing for the journey but a staff." (Mark 6:8, NRSV)

﹋ Intimate Friend,
You call us to journey with You
in the redemption of all humanity.
Give us your Holy Spirit
for a walking stick:
that, leaning on You alone
for our support,
we witness to the one Reality
that is needful,
even Jesus Christ our Friend
and our Redeemer. Amen.

Proper 16 (July 17–23)

ONE WHO FEEDS THE HUNGRY

- "Then [Jesus] took the five loaves and the two fish, raised his eyes to heaven and said the blessing; then he broke the loaves and began handing them to his disciples to distribute among the people.... They all ate as much as they wanted." (Mark 6:41–43, NJB)

﹋ One Who Feeds the Hungry,
as a mother answers the wail
of her child,
You sustain us through acts of love.

Increase our awareness
of our hunger for You:
that, knowing what we need,
we become more sensitive
to the needs of others;
Mother of All,
Bread of the World,
Spirit of Compassion.
Amen.

Alternative Prayer for Pentecost Proper 16 based on Mark
6:34: "Shepherdess of the Universe" (p. 90).

Proper 17 (July 24–30)

LOVER OF OUR BODIES AND SOULS

- After Jesus had fed them, "...the people said, 'This is indeed
  the prophet who is to come into the world.' Jesus, as he realised
  they were about to come and take him by force and make him
  king, fled back to the hills alone." (John 6:14–15, NJB)

   Lover of Our Bodies and Souls,
   in a world overwhelmed by division
   You draw the fragmented parts
   of ourselves into unity with You,
   and enlighten us with the wholeness
     of our being.
   Make us willing receivers
     of the Bread of Life:
   that, filled with the knowledge
     of your loving kindness,
   we embody the fullness
   which you have given us in Christ;

> Mother of All, Bread of Life,
> Cup that Overflows. Amen.

Alternative Prayer for Pentecost Proper 17 based on Mark 6:45–52 and John 6:1–21: "Storm-Goddess" (p. 72).

Proper 18 (July 31–August 6)

FRAGRANT BREAD

- "I am the bread of life. No one who comes to me will ever hunger...ever thirst." (John 6:35, NJB)

🙵 Fragrant Bread,
> your taste and smell arouse in us
> a longing to be one with You
>   and all creation
> and make holy the physical nature
>   of our spiritual journey.
> Use our hunger and thirst
>   to draw us to You:
> that, eating You,
> we become your presence to the world;
> Bakerwoman, Food of Life,
> Sustainer of Creation.
> Amen.

Proper 19 (August 7–13)

YOU WHO MOVE US BEYOND BIRTH TO BIRTH

- "Your [ancestors] ate manna in the desert and they are dead; but this is the bread which comes down from heaven, so that a person may eat it and not die." (John 6:49–51, NJB)

෧   You Who Move Us
    beyond birth to Birth,
    beyond water to Water,
    and beyond bread to Bread,
    You feed us with your wisdom.
    Carry us beyond rational understanding
        to complete trust in You:
    that we are no longer motivated
        by self-interest
    but live out our lives
    for the sake of all people;
    through Christ and in Christ
    by the movement of the Holy Spirit,
    world without end. Amen.

Proper 20 (August 14–20)

BREAST-FEEDING MOTHER[5]

- " ... whoever eats me will also draw life from me." (John 6:57,
  NJB)

෧   Womangod,
    as a mother breast-feeds her child,
    You have nourished us.
    Of your own body and blood
    You continually sustain us.
    Pour out for us the milk
        of your flowing Spirit:[6]

---

5. Mollenkott in *The Divine Feminine,* 20–25, cites the following sources from the Judeo-Christian tradition in which God is described as a Nursing Mother: Isaiah 49:15, 1 Peter 2:2–3, John 7:38, 2 Esdras 1:28–29, Clement of Alexandria, St. Augustine, and Teresa of Avila.

6. Mollenkott in *The Divine Feminine,* 23, cites Guerric of Igny who describes the Holy Spirit as milk from the breast of Mother Jesus.

that, in the example of Christ,
we grow in knowledge
    of your word and wisdom;
Nurturer and Supporter,
You are the Enabling One. Amen.

WOMANGOD AS QUEEN OF THE UNIVERSE (PROPERS 21–27)

General Prayer

HOLY GRANDMOTHER

☙   Holy Grandmother,
your eye upon us is kind,
and your advice gentle.
Always You affirm the good
    that is within us.
When we go astray, speak to us,
for in tender care
You nurture and inspire us,
and lead us to seek the Wisdom
    You have found;
Wise Old Woman,
Aspiring Maiden,
Spirit of Love. Amen.

Proper 21 (August 21–27)

LOVER OF CREATION

• "Be subject to one another out of reverence for Christ.... because we are members of his Body. 'For this reason a man will leave his father and mother and be joined to his wife, and the two will become one flesh.' " (Ephesians 5:21, 30–31, NRSV)

- " . . . for my flesh is true food and my blood is true drink." (John 6:55–69, NRSV)

❧ Lover of Creation,
  You are bone of our bone,
  and we are flesh of your flesh.
  Draw us into the warmth
      of your embrace,
  and whisper of your desire
      to be one with us:
  that, responding to your Passion,
  we become lovers with You
  of all the earth;
  Ardent Pursuer,
  Garden of Delight
  Spirit Who Inhabits this Earth. Amen.

Proper 22 (August 28–September 3)

GRANDMOTHER OF THE OPPRESSED

- "And [Jesus] said to them, 'How ingeniously you get round the commandment of God in order to preserve your own tradition!' " (Mark 7:9, NJB)

❧ Grandmother of the Oppressed,
  You delight in those who live
  out of hearts of compassion,
  and do not use law and religion
  to crush the spirits of the poor.
  Challenge us when we make decisions:
  that, reminded of your love for the world,

we seek to bring all people to your Way
  of justice and mercy;
Wise Old Woman,
Righteous One,
Spirit of Redemption. Amen.

Proper 23 (September 4–10)

HIDDEN TREASURE

- "My child, if you accept my words and treasure up my commandments within you, making your ear attentive to wisdom and inclining your heart to understanding....If you seek it like silver, and search for it as for hidden treasure, then you will...find the knowledge of God." (Proverbs 2:1–5, NRSV)

   Hidden Treasure,
    You nestle within a veil of mystery,
    and reserve your riches for those who seek
        until they find You.
    Lure us with your promise of abundance:
    that, discovering You, we share the wealth
        of your mercy throughout the earth;
    Elusive Jewel,
    One of Value,
    Source of Joy. Amen.

Alternative Prayer for Pentecost Proper 23 based on Mark
7:31–37: "Divine Healing Woman" (p. 92 and p. 102).

Proper 24 (September 11–17)

POTENT WINE

- "Then [Jesus] began to teach [the disciples] that the Son of man was destined to suffer grievously, ... and to be put to death, and after three days to rise again." (Mark 8:31–38, NJB)

☙   Potent Wine,
      You pour out your life that all may live.
      Fill us with the joy of your Passion:
      that, abandoning the shallow preoccupations
            of our lives,
      we dance with You in the Way of the Cross;
      Spendthrift Goddess,
      Overflowing Chalice,
      Ecstatic Spirit. Amen.

Proper 25 (September 18–24)

ONE WHO COMES IN LITTLE CHILDREN

- "Then he took a child and put it among them; and taking it in his arms, he said to them, 'Whoever welcomes one such child in my name welcomes me....'" (Mark 9:36–37, NRSV)

☙   One Who Comes to Us in Little Children,
      in those who are at greatest risk
      You seek our love,
      and in them open our eyes once more
      to the beauty and mystery of life.
      Pull the heartstrings of our consciences:
      that, remembering our own vulnerability,
      we care for those in need
            with speed and compassion;

Mother of All,
Child of Innocence,
Sustainer of Life. Amen.

Proper 26 (September 25–October 1)

HEART OF COMPASSION

- "Strengthen your hearts, for the coming of the Lord is near...
  and you have seen the purpose of the Lord, how the Lord is
  compassionate and merciful." (James 4:13–17; 5:7–11 NRSV)

 ∾ Heart of Compassion,
   in your throb we feel the pain
    of the world,
   and we weep with You at the wounds
    of our sisters and brothers.
   Make your love to move within us:
   that, freed of our addiction
    to comfort and safety,
   we commit our lives
   to empower the outcast and the oppressed,
   and to bring healing and joy to those You love;
   Center of the Universe,
   Crucified One,
   Wellspring of Joy. Amen.

COURAGE OF ESTHER

- Mordecai: "Who knows? Perhaps you have come to the throne
  for just such a time as this." Esther: "I shall go to the king in
  spite of the law; and if I perish, I perish." (Esther 4:12–17, NJB)

☙   Courage of Esther,
     You move in history
     to bring salvation to your people.
     Give us the strength
     to stand for justice
     even at the risk of our lives:
     that, letting go of those things
     that are less important,
     we participate in the building up
        of your eternal household;
     Queen of the Universe,
     One Who Gives Herself for Others,
     Spirit of Righteousness. Amen.

Proper 27 (October 2–8)

DIVINE WOMAN

• Compassion was the root of Jesus' response to the religious
  laws that allowed men to divorce their wives, potentially leav-
  ing them and their children destitute: "It was because you were
  so hard hearted that [Moses] wrote this commandment for
  you.... what God has united, human beings must not divide."[7]
  (Mark 10:2–16, NJB)

☙   Divine Woman,
     thrown away and left to die,

---

7. Ben Sira 25:23–26: "A bad wife brings humiliation, downcast looks, and a
wounded heart. Slack of hand and weak of knee is the man whose wife fails to make
him happy. Woman is the origin of sin, and it is through her that we all die. Do
not leave a leaky cistern to drop or allow a bad wife to say what she likes. If she
does not accept your control, divorce her and send her away" (quoted in Leonard
Swidler, *Biblical Affirmations of Woman* [Philadelphia: Westminster Press, 1979],
145). Swidler goes on to say that divorce in this tradition was expulsion from the
household and left women destitute. Divorce could be invoked for the most trivial
of reasons. In this context, Jesus' view on the indissolubility of marriage could be
understood as compassionate.

You call us to honor and protect
    every living being,
and to abhor violence in any form.
Teach us how to treasure one another:
that, faithful in body, mind, and soul,
we emulate your love for this world;
Wise Grandmother,
One Whose Love Is Enough,
Life-giving Spirit. Amen.

Harvest Thanksgiving

VINEYARD OF OUR DELIGHT

- "...the fig tree and vine give their full yield" (Joel 2:21–27, NRSV)

- "I would give you spiced wine to drink, the juice of my pomegranates." (Song of Solomon 8:2b, NRSV)

ዏ   Vineyard of Our Delight,
    You yield abundant fruit
        for all to share,
    and invite us into your chamber
        to feast and celebrate.
    Fill us with your passion
        to feed the world:
    that, leaving no one poor or hungry,
    all humanity dwell with You in peace;
    Source of Plenty,
    Staff of Life,
    Spirit of Generosity. Amen.

WOMANGOD AS ONE WHO BRINGS US HOME (PROPERS 28–REIGN OF CHRIST)

General Prayers

AUTUMN GODDESS

> ❧ Autumn Goddess,
> You make yourself known
> in the brilliance of fall leaves
> as they loosen their grip
> and prepare to let go.
> In the bite of the air
> as winter draws near,
> You speak to us of mortality.
> In this time of passage
> become once more our Midwife:
> that, strengthened by your nearness,
> we are born from this world to the next;
> Goddess of Life,
> Goddess of Death,
> Risen One. Amen.

WISE GRANDMOTHER

- Psalm 90:1, "Lord, you have been our dwelling place," suggests the refuge of God's bosom.

- Psalm 90:2, "Before the mountains were brought forth, or ever you had formed the earth and the world," suggests Sophia, who was before creation.

- Psalm 90:4, "A thousand years in your sight are like yesterday,...a watch in the night," takes up the theme of Sophia, manifestation of Divine Wisdom. (NRSV)

> ❧ Wise Grandmother,
> a thousand years in your sight
>   are like yesterday,
> and throughout time You have borne
> the pain of our hatred for ourselves
>   and one another.
> Open our eyes to ways those in power
>   have violated us,
> and reveal to us how we victimize others:
> that, shunning violence in any form,
> we participate in healing the chasm
>   of your woundedness.
> Old One Who Weeps for Us,
> Comforting Bosom,
> Dancing Spirit,
> You cry out for us. Amen.

Proper 28 (October 9–15)

ENTICING LIFESTREAM

- God: "Who told you that you were naked?" Adam: "It was the woman you put with me." (Genesis 3:9–12, NJB)

- "Teach us to count up the days that are ours, and we shall come to the heart of wisdom." (Psalm 90:12, NJB)

> ❧ Enticing Lifestream,
> earth cradles You in her valleys
> as You ripple over the pebbled ground
> of the garden of possibility.
> Carry us on the waters of the human quest:
> that, giving up our need to control,

we open to the process of your ongoing creation;
Grandmother,
Sister in Wisdom,
Moistening One. Amen.

Alternative Prayer for Pentecost Proper 28 based on Mark
10:17–30: "Hidden Treasure" (p. 111)

- "Jesus, looking at [the rich man], loved him and said, 'You lack
  one thing; go, sell what you own, and give the money to the
  poor, and you will have treasure in heaven.'" (Mark 10:21,
  NRSV)

Proper 29 (October 16–22)

ONE WHO SPEAKS TO US IN OUR BROKENNESS

- "Ill-treated and afflicted, he never opened his mouth." (Isaiah
  53:7, NJB)
- "Before being in the image of either Eve or Mary, womansoul is
  in the image of Psyche. It is our return to Psyche as WomanChrist
  that can heal the victimizing dualism that has become a part of
  Christian imagery over the centuries." (Christin L. Weber[8])

☙   One Who Speaks to Us
      in our brokenness,
      in taking the role of Victim,
      You join all who suffer abuse,
      and You share our pain.
      Open us to our own woundedness:
      that, released by the strength
          of our anger,
      we find the courage to seek justice

8. Christin Lore Weber, "Releasing the Victim," *WomanChrist: A New Vision of
Feminist Spirituality* (San Francisco: Harper & Row, 1985), 88.

for ourselves and others:
Redemptress of the Afflicted,
Soul-Sister,
Compassionate Healer. Amen.

Proper 30 (October 23–29)

LIBERATOR OF THE DISPOSSESSED

- "Watch, I shall bring them back from the land of the north and gather them in from the far ends of the earth. . . . I shall guide them to streams of water, by a smooth path where they will not stumble." (Jeremiah 31:8–9, NJB)

✸   Liberator of the Dispossessed,
     You look with pity on the victims
         of this world,
     and restore them to the fortune
         of original blessing.[9]
     Make your steadfast love to well up in us:
     that, ministering to those who are afflicted,
     we come to know You as our deepest truth.
     Lady of the Four Winds,
     Child of Innocence,
     Beckoning Spirit,
     we follow You with weeping and laughter
         and shouts of joy. Amen.

---

9. For the concept of "original blessing," see Matthew Fox, *Original Blessing: A Primer in Creation Spirituality* (Santa Fe: Bear & Company, 1983), 42–56.

Proper 31 (October 30–November 5)

AUTHOR OF LOVE

- Deuteronomy 6:1–9 instructs the people to teach the Great Commandment to their children, to bind it as a sign on their hands, and to immerse themselves in its meaning.
- In Mark 12:28–34 Jesus cites entrance into the reign of God as connected to obedience to the first commandment.

> ❧ Author of Love,
> You write your law of compassion
>   in the Book of Life,
> and share with us your longing
> for a bond of trust with your people.
> Inscribe in our hearts
> the story of your saving actions:
> that, entering the drama
>   of your redemption of the world,
> we seek to bring all people
>   into unity and peace with You;
> Heavenly Scribe,
> Divine Word,
> Poet of Justice. Amen.

All Saints' Day

DIVINE GRANDMOTHER

> ❧ Divine Grandmother,
> You plant all souls
> in this garden earth,
> and nurture each seed
> that we may grow and flourish.

At the time of harvest,
collect us into the folds
of your starch-scented apron,
and stir us into the fragrant goodness
of the bread that You bake:
that, returning to You,
we join the women and men
who have ever served You
with faithfulness and love
    throughout all time.
Great Ancestress,
Risen One,
You shine on us in Glory forever.
Amen.

Proper 32 (November 6–12)

PETULANT GRANDMOTHER

- "A poor widow came and put in two small coins.... 'In truth
  I tell you, this poor widow has put more in than all who have
  contributed to the treasury; for they have all put in money they
  could spare, but she in her poverty has put in everything she
  possessed....'" (Mark 12:4–44, NJB)

❧   Petulant Grandmother,
     You demand that we give all that we have,
     and You do not rest until we become
     all that You intend us to be.
     Goad us into the realization
     that life is your gift to us:
     that, laying aside those things
         that are unimportant,
     we grasp what is good and true and beautiful.

For You are the Thorn in Our Sides,
the Impetuous Child,
and the One Who Stirs Us Up—
the Holy One from whom we draw life
and hope and wisdom. Amen.

Proper 33 (November 13–19)

ANCIENT WOMAN

- "Daniel said, 'I have been seeing visions in the night. . . . thrones
  were set in place and one most venerable took his seat. His robe
  was white as snow.' " (Daniel 7:2, 9, NJB)

☙   Ancient Woman,
      You spin out creation
      on the Wheel of Life,
      and our beginning and end
      feel the rough skin of your hands.
      When the sun fails
      and the moon goes dark,
      gather your children
      from the ends of the earth:
      that, redeemed by your compassion,
      all humanity enter the home
      that You have prepared for us;
      Lady of the Four Winds,
      Uniter of Heaven and Earth,
      One Who Brings Us Home. Amen.

Proper 34 (Reign of Christ)

QUEEN OF THE UNIVERSE

- " 'I am the Alpha and the Omega,' says the Lord God, who is, who was, and who is to come." (Revelation 1:8, NJB)[10]

   Queen of the Universe,
   in your acts of healing and justice
   You unite heaven and earth
   and make us one with You.
   Open before us the passage into Shalom:
   that the first shall be last
      and the last first;
   for You are Earth-Bearer,
   Wellspring of Hope,
   Purifying Fire,
   and Gate of Heaven,
   the Most Blessed One,
   now and forever. Amen.

   Queen of the Universe,
   You wrap the world in robes of crimson,
   that all might keep the final feast.
   As we drift in your arms to Shalom, our home,
   the scent of your kiss is spicy
      like a bouquet of dried flowers,
   memories of lilies and the honeysuckle vine.
   Make us one with heaven and with earth:

---

10. The title "Queen of Heaven and Earth," an image of wholeness similar to that of alpha and omega, has been used to venerate Mary, the mother of Jesus (see above p. 20). Like Christ, the Queen of the Universe has descended through death into the underworld and has ascended again to rule over all that is. See Sylvia B. Perera, *Descent to the Goddess* (Toronto: Inner City Books, 1981). It is the Goddess who carries us across the threshold into our eternal home, and She who welcomes us into our true selves in unity of body, mind, and spirit.

that peace and joy last forever.
Woman of Wholeness,
as we become one with You,
we celebrate all that we are
and all that in You we shall become;
world without end, alleluia! Amen.

Bibliography

Bernard of Clairvaux, Saint. *On the Love of God.* Translated from the French by a Religious of C.S.M.V. London: A. R. Mowbray & Co., 1961.

Bozarth-Campbell, Alla, "Bakerwoman." In LaVonne Althouse and Lois K. Snook, eds. *In God's Image: Toward Wholeness for Women and Men,* Division for Mission in North America, Lutheran Church in America, 1976.

Christ, Carol, and Judith Plaskow, eds. *Womanspirit Rising: A Feminist Reader.* San Francisco: Harper & Row, 1979.

Clark, Linda, Marian Ronan, and Eleanor Walker. *Image-Breaking Image-Building: A Handbook for Creative Worship with Women of Christian Tradition.* New York: Pilgrim Press, 1981.

Doyle, Brendan, ed. *Meditations with Julian of Norwich.* Santa Fe: Bear & Company, 1983.

Engelsman, Joan Chamberlain. *The Feminine Dimension of the Divine.* Philadelphia: Westminster Press, 1979.

Hughes, Helen Kathleen. "The Opening Prayer of the Sacramentary: A Structural Study of the Easter Cycle." Dissertation, University of Notre Dame. Ann Arbor, Mich.: University Microfilms International, 1981.

Johnson, Elizabeth A. *She Who Is: The Mystery of God in Feminist Theological Discourse.* New York: Crossroad, 1992.

Lawrence, Caleb. "Third Sunday after Epiphany." In Joyce Carlson, ed. *Journey: Stories and Prayers for the Christian Year from the People of the First Nations.* Toronto: Anglican Book Centre, 1991.

Mariechild, Diane. *Mother Wit: A Feminist Guide to Psychic Development.* Trumansburg, N.Y.: Crossing Press, 1981.

McFague, Sallie. *Metaphorical Theology: Models of God in Religious Language.* Philadelphia: Fortress Press, 1982.

Mechtild of Magdeburg. "How the Soul Speaks to God." In Fiona Bowie, ed. *Beguine Spirituality: An Anthology.* London: SPCK, 1989.

Miller, Jean Baker. *Toward a New Psychology of Women.* Boston: Beacon Press, 1976.

Mitchell, Stephen. *The Gospel according to Jesus: A New Translation and Guide to His Essential Teachings for Believers and Unbelievers.* New York: HarperCollins, 1991.

Mollenkott, Virginia Ramey. *The Divine Feminine: The Biblical Imagery of God as Female.* New York: Crossroad, 1984.

Moltmann-Wendel, Elisabeth. *The Women around Jesus.* London: SCM Press, 1982.

Pagels, Elaine. *The Gnostic Gospels.* New York: Random House, 1979.

Patai, Rafael. *The Hebrew Goddess.* New York: KTAV, 1967.

Procter-Smith, Marjorie. *In Her Own Rite: Constructing Feminist Liturgical Tradition.* Nashville: Abingdon Press, 1990.

Saiving, Valerie. "The Human Situation: A Feminine View." In Carol Christ and Judith Plaskow, eds. *Womanspirit Rising: A Feminist Reader.* San Francisco: Harper & Row, 1979.

Schüssler Fiorenza, Elisabeth. *In Memory of Her: A Feminist Theological Reconstruction of Christian Origins.* New York: Crossroad, 1984.

Stone, Merlin. *When God Was a Woman.* New York: Harcourt Brace Jovanovich, 1976.

Swidler, Leonard. *Biblical Affirmations of Woman.* Philadelphia: Westminster Press, 1979.

Tillich, Paul. *Systematic Theology,* vol. 1. Chicago: University of Chicago Press, 1951.

Trible, Phyllis. *God and the Rhetoric of Sexuality.* Philadelphia: Fortress Press, 1978.

Uhlein, Gabriele, ed. *Meditations on Hildegard of Bingen.* Santa Fe: Bear & Company, 1982.

Washbourn, Penelope. *Becoming Woman: The Quest for Wholeness in Female Experience.* New York: Harper & Row, 1977.

Weber, Christin Lore. *WomanChrist: A New Vision of Feminist Spirituality.* San Francisco: Harper & Row, 1985.

Index of Biblical References

— ❧ —

— OLD TESTAMENT —

Genesis
1:1–5	47
3:9–12	117
9:11	68
9:14–15	68
17:15–19	69
29:9	90

Exodus
2:16–21	90
3:4	97
20:1–17	70
24:8	80
28	92

Leviticus
19:18	63

Deuteronomy
6:1–9	120
18:18	60
32:11–12	56
32:18	48

1 Samuel
3:10	58

2 Samuel
6:2	101
7:10	48

2 Kings
5:1–14	62

2 Chronicles
36:15–16	71
36:17–19	72

Esther
4:12–17	113

Job
7:3, 6	61

Psalms
19:7	70
23	90
41:1	63
51:10	73
57:1 and 8	99
62:6	59
63:6–7	58
63:7	56
90:1, 2, 4	116
90:12	117
97:1, 8, 11	51
98:1–2, 4–8	91
111:10	60
114:7–8	85
147:1–4	61
147:4	58

Proverbs _____
1:20, 23	70
2:1–5	111
31	50
31:10–31	52

Song of Solomon _____
3:1	45
5:1	103
8:2b	115

Isaiah _____
9:4–6	51
40:4–5	46
43:18–20	96
43:19a	63
53:7	118
62:6–7, 10–12	50
63:15	45
64:1–9	46

Jeremiah _____
17:7–8	79
31:8–9	119

Ezekiel _____
37:4	96

Daniel _____
7:2, 9	122

Hosea _____
2:14–23	103

Joel _____
2:1, 10; 4:18	67
2:21–27	115

— NEW TESTAMENT —

Matthew _____
5:44, 48	63
6:3, 17	66
13:33	46
27:57–61	82

Mark _____
1:8	58
1:12	69
1:14–20	60
1:17–18	56
1:22	60
1:30–34	61
1:40	62
2:5–12	63
4:30–34	100
4:35–41	101
4:37, 39	101
5: 21–43	102
6:1–6	104
6:8	105
6:34	90, 106
6:41–43	105
6:45–52	107
7:9	110
7:31–37	111
8:31–38	70, 112
9:1–7	62
9:2–8	70
9:36–37	112
10:2–16	114
10:17–30	118
10:21	118
11:12–14	77
12:28–34	120
12:4–44	121
14:1, 3–9	78
14:50	81

14:72	*81*
15:37–38	*76*
15:40–41	*81*
15:45–47	*82*
16:1–8	*88*

Luke

1:35	*48*
2:36–38	*53*
13:20–21	*46*
13:34	*57*
24:35–48	*89*

John

1:1	*52*
1:1–18	*54, 54*
1:8–9	*47*
3:16	*71*
6:1–21	*107*
6:14–15	*106*
6:35	*107*
6:49–51	*107*
6:55–69	*110*
6:57	*108*
10:11–18	*90*
12:24	*73*
12:27	*73*
12:27–36	*79*
15:1–8	*90*
15:13	*91*
17:11b–19	*92*
20:16, 18	*86*
20:19	*88*

Acts

2:1	*96*
4:32	*88*

Romans

4:19–25	*69*
6:3–11	*85*

1 Corinthians

10:16–17	*80*

2 Corinthians

4:13–18	*99*
4:16–18	*99*
4:6	*98*
5:17	*100*
12:7–9	*64*

Ephesians

1:3	*105*
1:3–4	*54*
1:8–10	*93*
3:8–9	*58*
5:21, 30–31	*109*

Hebrews

5:7–8	*73*

James

4:13–17	*113*
5:7–11	*113*

Revelation

1:8	*123*